Sarah and After

Sarah
and After

Five Women Who Founded a Nation

————◆————

LYNNE REID BANKS

Doubleday & Company, Inc.
Garden City, New York

ISBN 0-385-11456-7 Trade
0-385-11455-9 Prebound
Library of Congress Catalog Card Number 76–16250

For my neglected goddaughters
KATE BENFIELD and KATHARINE AYTON
lest they, like many of their contemporaries,
grow up believing that the Christian religion
sprang up without roots in the year 1.

CONTENTS

One
Sarah and Hagar
1

Two
Rebecca
49

Three
Leah and Rachel
99

Four
Dinah
139

One

———◆———

Sarah and Hagar

It was unbearably hot and stuffy inside the basket. Sarai could neither lie nor sit in it in comfort—it had not been made to hold a human body, but grain. She did sit, but with her knees drawn up and her shoulders bent at an unnatural angle, with the lid pressed down on her neck and head. Crushed and sweltering, as much in fear as from the heat, she crouched like this, while the jogging gait of the two asses which carried her basket between them made her feel more and more ill.

She was a patient girl—she had been bred and trained to a role of patience and submission. She had accepted unquestioningly her husband Abram's plan to pass her off as his sister while they were in Egypt. Of course she had heard how wicked and immoral the Egyptians were, how they had only to see a beautiful foreign woman to be ready to murder her menfolk in order to carry her off. If they knew she was married to Abram, they would surely kill him—so Abram had told her.

It had pleased her secretly to learn from him that she was so beautiful that no man could resist her. She adored her husband; the thought of anything happening to him terrified her far more than any threat to herself, or even to her honor. As to that, surely Abram's God would protect her?

She had no personal knowledge of this great Being

who ruled her husband's actions, and whose commands had sent them all from their houses and families in Ur of the Chaldees, so long ago. What Sarai knew of this god, she feared. But Abram believed in Him absolutely, and Sarai believed absolutely in Abram.

Nevertheless, her thirst was becoming desperate.

"Husband—" she whispered humbly, next time she felt Abram's shadow fall on the basket.

"Brother," he corrected. "What is it? Are you very hot?"

"And thirsty," she said. "I am sick from the dancing of these hateful asses. Are we not within sight of Egypt?"

"Yes. Soon the Pharaoh's guard should ride out to meet us. If you are discovered, do you know what to do?"

"I'll say we are brother and sister, just as you told me. Now may I have some water?"

The asses jerked to a stop. The top of the basket was unfastened and her head was free. She felt dizzy at first; but, hearing the blessed sound of water being poured, she eased her head upward, feeling the sun fall on her face like a hammer blow.

Near her stood the untidy jumble of the small caravan. The few asses were thin and panting from the heat, and from hunger, for they had recently fled from a place of famine. Her husband's nephew, Lot, and his wife and daughters were a sad sight, hollow-cheeked, filthy, and weary. Some of the daughters threw sullen, envious glances at Sarai because she was allowed to ride—Sarai almost laughed, thinking how much she would prefer to walk, free and unafraid as they were. She could easily have cursed her beauty and wished herself plain and ordinary, no danger to herself or her husband. . . .

A cup was offered to her. She grabbed it eagerly and felt a wild, sensual delight as the water ran over her parched tongue. A few drops cut a path through the grain dust on her chin and downward, a delicious, cold trickle. . . . When the cup was drained, she pushed back the black coils of her hair and rearranged the scarf over it, feeling that now no trial would be too hard for her.

Suddenly the beasts raised their drooping ears and gazed to the south. Lot, who was mounted, immediately shaded his eyes.

"Men are coming," he said shortly.

At once all was bustle. Sarai was crammed back into the basket, while Lot's wife hastily drew veils over the faces of her daughters. Then the caravan slowly resumed its way.

Sarai, in her dim, jerking prison, clenched her hands and tried not to tremble. "The Lord will defend you," Abram had said. But how could an invisible god come between a defenseless woman and a brutal man? Would a magic shield spring up to part them, or would the man be struck dead? Sarai was shocked at her own cowardice. She had thought she could face anything for Abram. But she was young and excited by life, and now that she could hear the shouts of the Egyptians she almost wished she had never married this strange, god-driven husband, that she were a virgin again, safe in her father's house in Ur.

The caravan stopped. The Egyptians' voices were coarse and brutish. She heard one, who was evidently an official, rasping out questions and commands. He was assessing the tax they would have to pay on their goods before entering Egypt. At last he reached Sarai's basket.

"What's in here?"

"Barley," said Abram.

"Are you sure it isn't wheat?"

Abram hesitated, and then said, "You wish me to pay the tax on wheat?"

"You need only pay on the contents. It's pepper, perhaps?"

"We do not carry pepper. But I'm willing to pay as if it were."

There was a sudden lurch as the man heaved up the basket in his arms. Sarai bit back a gasp.

"It is indeed far too heavy to be pepper," said the tax inspector, now in tones of active suspicion. "No wonder you are so willing to pay the pepper tax if it's gold!"

"I will pay the tax on gold," said Abram.

Sarai could hardly restrain her panicky irritation. *Oh, foolish husband!* she thought. *Why didn't you refuse to pay the wheat tax, like any ordinary man?*

"Is no charge I can put on you too high?" roared the officer. "In that case I must see for myself! It must contain precious stones."

A bronze spear pierced the side of the lid, just grazing Sarai's shoulder, and the lid was prized off. Sarai cowered, but rough hands hauled her out in a flurry of soft damp veils and beads and bare feet, for her sandals got left behind in the basket.

She pranced in pain on the fiery sand before the officer, with her hands up to her face. Without hesitation he took both her wrists in one hard hand and dragged them down; then he pulled back her head by the hair, so that the sun fell on her shamefully exposed face.

A gasp of incredulity issued like a serpent's hiss from a dozen male throats. Sarai felt the grasp on her wrists and hair fall away and, daring to open her eyes a slit, looked at the officer. He had a dark, sensuous face with black eyes full of greed and savagery. But at that momnet there was no lust in his expression, only wonder and admiration.

"A jewel indeed," he whispered gratingly, and his tongue stuck out between his lips. Then, recovering himself, he turned to Abram.

"Is this woman yours?" he asked.

"She is my—sister," Abram said slowly.

"Why was she hidden?"

"To save you from temptation, and her from dishonor."

"It is no dishonor for any woman to be offered to the Pharaoh," said another officer. The men exchanged glances of regret. Clearly they wanted her for themselves, but such a beauty was fit only for the king himself.

Abram put his hand out to Sarai, and she saw that *he* trembled now. "She is of my family! I do not wish to dispose of her."

"You have no choice," said the officer. "You are fortunate. For such beauty as hers, you will no doubt be rewarded beyond your dreams. Pack up your goods again and follow us. The woman rides with me."

The next moment Sarai found herself lifted onto the officer's camel. The man mounted behind her, pulled the beast's head around, and jogged off before she had time to do more than glance despairingly at Abram, who stood in the sand gazing after her as if stunned.

The palace of the Pharaoh was, to Sarai, a marvel so fabulous that all her fears were, for the time being, lost in wonder.

Her life had been lived in nomadic primitivity. She was used to low stone buildings, or desert tents made of black goat skins; fires built on the ground between stones; water laboriously drawn from wells. The only smells she knew were those of dust and dung and sweat and scorching flour. She knew nothing of spacious architecture or decorated walls, of fine garments embroidered with threads of gold, of sweet, heady perfumes, or of beautiful jewelry and artifacts made of glass and precious metals.

Nor did she in the least understand what was happening when she was taken to the women's quarters of the palace and, in a room quite huge in her eyes and brilliantly inlaid with different-colored stone, stripped of her coarse, travel-stained clothes and gently pushed down some steps into a big stone trough filled with water. She thought at first they wanted to drown her!

But then for the first time in her life she felt cool,

clean water lapping her right up to her neck. She was washed all over, and then, dry and clean, she was rubbed with oils smelling so sweet they made her feel faint. When they dressed her again, it was in a loose-sleeved robe of such fine thread that she felt she was wearing nothing at all, and her hair, with every speck of dust and oil washed out of it, was draped in a veil bordered with gold. When finally her neck and arms hung with gold and turquoise and silver, she felt her own body so strange to her that she lost the sense of herself as the simple, obedient, desert-bred wife of Abram.

And when at last, with much laughter, the woman attending her stood her up before a panel of polished metal and let her see her reflection full-length for the first time, there came a moment of pure—or impure—sensation that she would never forget (nor, in later years, forgive herself for). It was a moment of total, intoxicating vanity, and total, guiltless joy. For she was indeed a great beauty; her beauty inflamed even herself with a passion and a sense of power that took her by storm and made her cry out with sudden rapture as she gazed at herself.

Then she was led before Pharaoh.

His room was like a marble forest. Huge pillars of stone shaped like towers of reeds ranged about awesomely. Gold and jewels shone everywhere—the jugs of wine, the bowls of fruit, the hems of garments, and the personal ornaments were all of gold. The king himself lay on the floor on brilliant rugs, surrounded by attendants. Sarai was unable to resist one quick look at him before casting her eyes modestly to the tiles at her feet; but that look was enough to bring all her terrors rushing back upon her.

He was a small man, swarthy and simian, with a long nose curved and sharp-ridged, and a strangely cut black beard. The beards of her own people were always left untrimmed; Abram's, already gray, was soft and flowing. This man's looked like a spearhead with the point cut off.

Everything about him was, to Sarai, alien, ugly, and terrifying. In some strange way, she was relieved. . . .

"Unveil her."

The women on each side lifted away the diaphanous scarf that had covered her hair and face. Sarai, who had kept herself veiled even from Abram for months after their marriage, was so deeply ashamed that she couldn't keep her feet, and fell down on the floor to conceal her face. But she was ruthlessly lifted up and placed—naked as it seemed to her, though only her face was exposed—at the Pharaoh's feet.

There was absolute silence throughout the vast room as he gazed at her. She lay with clenched hands and senses benumbed with humiliation and distress. Her only conscious thought was a question: was the god of Abram, far from protecting her, bent on punishing her for some unknown sin? Why else should he let her suffer this hideous shame, instead of reaching out a merciful hand to shield her face from the eyes of this repulsive stranger?

The Pharaoh straightened himself and clapped his hands sharply.

"Leave us."

There came a whisper of many feet stroking the tiles, loud at first, then softer to silence, while Sarai lay in the grasp of apprehension. For the first time, doubt and disloyalty entered her terrified thoughts. How could Abram allow this? Why had he not fought for her? He had trusted his God to protect *her*. If Abram had shown more valor, might *he* not then have deserved his God's protection? And now the hand of the Pharaoh was upon her, and she was speechless with horror, burying her unveiled face in her hands and catching her breath in little broken gasps.

O God of my husband—

The prayer was her first, silent and despairing. It went no further.

The hand was gone.

She cowered, unbelieving. There came a grunting sound, halfway between the cough of an angry ape and a cry of dismay. She dared to peep through her fingers, and saw that the king was staring—not at her, but at the hand he had laid on her, a hand suddenly shaking like an old man's. A crawling whiteness had come upon it, as if the skin were dying. Even as Sarai looked, it spread.

The Pharaoh leaped to his feet, Sarai forgotten, and began running about distractedly, rubbing the leprous hand and crying out in disgust. Slaves appeared among the pillars, and hurried to help him. But suddenly there were more cries, and the slaves too, and then the king's women, and his attendants, began to appear, running about in panic. Sarai, gaping, saw the white diseased patches spreading on the swarthy bodies of her oppressors.

It was some days before Sarai, shaken but unharmed, was restored to Abram. But a great deal had changed. The Pharaoh had changed, from an all-powerful tyrant into a shriveled, terror-stricken, obsequious benefactor. His sudden visitation had been lifted—his body was whole again; but he was a broken man, for he had seen the power of Abram's God and all his intent now was to placate Abram and get him out of Egypt. To this end, he heaped him with gifts. Not only great herds of sheep, asses, and even camels, enough to transform Abram (and Lot too, for the Pharaoh was taking no chances) into a rich man; but gifts of grain and gold as well, and other provisions enough to see them safely through any journey, even if they traveled back to Canaan where the famine was still raging.

Abram was very subdued as they left Egypt, speeded by outriders whom the Pharaoh had charged with seeing them well and far on their way. Sarai walked alongside and a little behind her husband. She frowned with concentration. She was trying to project herself into his thoughts, to understand what was troubling him. Perhaps his God was talking to him? She realized that she, as a mere female, had no hope of ever being in direct touch with this Being who had saved her with such a fearful display of His power. She was quite bemused when she thought of it—herself saved; Pharaoh humbled; Abram made rich . . . and she with him, for had she not been given a handmaiden of her very own? And no ordinary girl at that, for the beautiful creature walking deferentially behind her at this moment was none other than Pharaoh's own daughter, Hagar.

She had not, of course, been part of the consignment of servants that Pharaoh had given to Abram and Lot. But suddenly, at the last moment, this princess had stepped forward from beside her father and thrown herself at Abram's feet.

"This man is the servant of the true God," she said. "Let me rather be a servant of God's servant, than a princess in a land of false gods."

Abram, walking at the head of his newly enriched caravan, was not communicating with God. He was struggling with his conscience.

God had not ordered him to pass Sarai off as his sister; that had been entirely his own idea. And now, when Abram secretly felt he should be suffering some punishment, even if it were only Pharaoh's wrath for his deception and not some plague sent by God for his sinfulness in putting his wife in danger, he found himself not merely safe but rewarded with riches beyond his dreams.

His shame at his cowardice burned him, but far worse was the sense of spiritual degradation he felt on reflecting that he might as well have sold Sarai's honor for all these herds and treasure which surrounded him. He raised his head, and with stabbing pangs of inner pain surveyed the reward of his wicked weakness—a sea of bobbing horns, the pattering of a thousand hoofs; bales and baskets loaded onto the draft animals; and men and women servants, lavished on him by the frantic Pharaoh so that his new wealth would not be a burden to him.

But it was. Every sheep, every measure of good wheat and barley, every gold ornament and silver coin lay upon his heart like a stone. And, feeling this pain, he suddenly understood—this was God's way of punishing him. He heaved a deep sigh, accepting it, and reached back his hand to touch Sarai in gratitude so strong it was like a knife in his chest.

A long, difficult journey brought them back to the foot of the mountain, near Beit-El, where Abram had raised an altar to God on his outward journey, and there they settled for a while, Abram and Lot and their families and herds and servants together.

The famine was past, and there was plentiful grazing again. The herds and flocks increased; the men and women servants formed families, and soon there were almost as many children in the settlement as young lambs. And there came a time, inevitably, when the grazing became exhausted and there was not enough room for all Abram's and all Lot's people to share the same ground.

The quarrels began among the herdsmen and spread to the heads of the families. To save strife, Abram told Lot to choose any route he liked and lead his families and herds away in that direction, while Abram would choose some other. So Lot chose to go to the southeast, where he could see a fertile plain near the Jordan River.

"Go then," said Abram, "with God's blessing."

"I do not need your God," said Lot, for he still felt bitter about the grazing quarrel.

"You will need Him," said Abram quietly. "In the direction you have chosen lie Sodom and other wicked cities, where heathens worship their idols and where no righteousness is. In such a place, a good man might be eaten alive by evil, if God were not with him."

Lot masked his unease with a sneering smile.

"We leave tomorrow."

Sarai sat at her tent flap and watched them go.

A heavy sadness settled on her with the falling dust raised by their passing. The sun was setting, reddening the pink, round, naked hills beyond the Jordan. The clouds of dust rose against the sky, thickening the pure clear air; the tinkling of the herd bells and the half tones of the herdsmen's reed flutes drifted back to her more and more faintly.

She didn't know why she should feel so bereft. She hadn't really liked Lot. Her own people were still about her, and her husband's herds, and all the evidence of his wealth to give as much security and continuity as there could ever be in the wandering life of a nomadic woman. And yet the tinkling bells, the eyes of her women sitting near her, the very motes of dust settling through the red rays of the sun, all saddened and disquieted her.

She sighed heavily as the last herdboy vanished over a knuckle of rock and the sounds of the flocks died into silence. Looking around, she saw their own herds, settling down, munching, for the cool coming of the night, and found that, far from comforting her, they disturbed her more than ever. How their numbers had increased since they came out of Egypt! And not only the beasts. Wandering among them was a young girl, little more than a child herself, holding her first baby closely to her hip. Other women sat suckling their little ones in the openings of their tents, content to catch the cool evening wind on their breasts. . . . Sarai turned her eyes away with a sharp pain in her own breast, and caught Hagar looking at her. Hagar had not married. At least there was one woman about Sarai who also had no child. And yet . . . Was there mockery, even there?

Late that night Abram, who had ridden out to see Lot on his way, returned. He found Sarai still sitting outside in the darkness, a small fire which she had kindled to keep out the piercing mountain cold flickering on her face. It showed the new shadows that had come there, and the drawn lines of a new sorrow.

He sat beside her and she half rose to bring him a drink.

"Let Hagar serve me," he said. "Tonight I have things to say to you."

Sarai called softly, and Hagar, sleepy-eyed and swathing her hair, padded into the firelight with a jug of fresh milk. She served Abram, then vanished again.

Abram did not drink. He lit a torch in the fire and held it up to look at Sarai. "Have you been sitting here since we all left?"

"Yes."

"You are coated in dust. Even your hair and your eyelashes look white."

"Soon they will be white in truth," she said quietly.

But he did not hear. His eyes were burning, and when he took her hand and held it, back uppermost, in his, she could feel his trembling.

"Wife," he said softly. "Do you see this layer of dust upon your hand? Could you count the motes that are here, or those on your little finger alone?" Puzzled, she shook her head. "Could you count the grains of dust upon your smallest nail, or upon one eyelash? But Sarai, listen to me, our children and those that spring from them shall be *as the dust of the earth*."

Sarai sat straight, poised, tense. Her eyes were fixed unblinkingly on his, and her breath came short.

"Our children?" she whispered at last. "Did your God tell you this?"

"This and much more. All this land will belong to our descendants. . . . But this much concerns you, my patient, good, and gentle wife. Do not doubt or grieve. Your time will come. It has been promised."

"Then—then you will not put me aside for child-lessness?" she said, voicing her own worst terror.

"It has been promised," Abram repeated. They gazed at each other raptly in the firelight, and then he gathered her in his arms and took her into the tent.

On the dark verge of the firelight, Hagar stood tall and unmoving for a long time before going quietly to collect the untouched milk and heap stones on the fire.

Soon after Lot's departure, Abram's family shifted their grazing grounds too. They moved south, after the fashion of nomads, going slowly and pitching their tents for weeks at a time as they went, until they reached a fertile plain near Hebron, and there the land was so accommodating that they settled. Abram built a new altar to the Lord as a sign that this place was to be their home for some time.

The life of a wanderer is hard on a woman. The constant pressure of the sun and the abrasive sting of the sands, the variable winds and the alternations of daytime heat and nighttime cold dry out the skin and draw the bright life from the eyes and hair. And for Sarai it was doubly hard, for her spirit was drying up with her body, drying up from disappointment, from hope continually renewed and continually confounded. To see the meanest creatures about her repeatedly and effortlessly producing new life and to be forever aware of her own emptiness was an afflic-tion more terrible than any disease or punishment. She thought, often and ever more bitterly, of God's promise, which, as she aged, grew less and less possible of ful-fillment; she felt herself unjustly cursed, the more so since her hopes had been raised so high.

As the years passed, she grew more and more silent and withdrawn, and her intimate conversations with her husband dwindled to a simple exchange of domestic necessities. Abram was so absorbed with the inner world he shared with his God that he scarcely noticed her distress; in any case his faith was so great that he would not have countenanced the reason for it. He never saw how old she was getting, any more than he was aware of his own wrinkled, leathery face and withered hands and lamb-white hair and beard. His bearing was still straight and vigorous and he still walked without a stick.

One day a messenger came running into their camp. Lot had been captured and carried off to the north by the armies of some warrior-kings who had invaded Sodom, the town where Lot, despite Abram's warnings, had chosen to live. Abram, alarmed by the boldness of the invaders and afraid for his own flocks and household, which were rich enough to attract any plunderer, rounded up a small force from among his own people and hurried off to rescue Lot and deal a blow to the invaders. It was the first time in his life that he had done any fighting, and Sarai flew into a passion of anxiety, pacing about in her tent and wringing her hands.

"At his age, and with no experience!" she cried to Hagar, who sat, calm and watchful as ever, kneading dough upon the stone floor.

"Why should you fear, mistress?" she said, raising her great olive-black eyes to Sarai. "God must preserve him to fulfill his destiny."

Sarai stopped pacing and stared at her.

"What do you know of his destiny?" she asked shrilly.

Hagar dropped her eyes again, and her slim hands and still-slender, youthful body continued the sensuous movements of kneading the dough.

"When a woman lives close to a man," she said

slowly, "even as his wife's slave, she learns much. Did not his God promise him that He would multiply his descendants 'till they were like the dust of the earth'? How can that happen if my master should die now in battle before he has a son?"

Sarai was speechless, not only with surprise at Hagar's knowing all this, but with some stronger emotion, which worked in her like yeast and quickly swelled into fury. It was intolerable that this woman, still young enough to bear a child, should touch even so indirectly upon the bitter burden on Sarai's aging heart.

"Get out of my sight!" she screamed. "You are impertinent! What dare a slave know? Get away from me!"

Hagar quietly stood up and left the tent with downcast eyes. It was the first time she had ever seen Sarai angry, and she was afraid of her; but once outside in the sunlight she stretched her body and threw out her arms to the dung-tainted wind. "What do I care what she says?" she thought before she could control herself. "She is so much older than I . . ."

Sarai, watching from inside the tent, saw the free, youthful gesture and clutched her own forearms suddenly, digging the nails into the shriveled flesh. Guilt and shame crawled over her like the leprosy of the Pharaoh long ago. She was taken by a sudden loathing for herself, for her own aged, barren body. She began to beat her shrunken breast and sob aloud with wretchedness.

But she hid her misery from Abram when he returned, quite safe and with his reputation greatly enhanced, from the victorious encounter. Eagerly, like a boy, he regaled her with stories of the battle, how he had brought Lot safely back from Dan and won over the invading kings by refusing to take loot or compensation. And soon she saw that he was again in communication with God, for he spent long hours walking alone on the mountain, returning with renewed and ever more grandiose promises for their nonexistent descendants.

In growing secret disbelief, Sarai listened. Those who came after them would be as numerous as the stars in the night sky; they would be slaves in a foreign country for four hundred years, and then would be led out of bondage and given huge tracts of land—all that lay between the great river of Egypt and the Euphrates, far to the north.

The bitterness rose to choke her as she thought how this news would have brought pride and dignity to her soul, if only she saw the faintest likelihood of its coming true. "How can any of this be," she cried out at last, "when we are slipping into our graves childless?"

"We shall have children," Abram said firmly. "Do not doubt it. It has been promised to me."

"To *you*, yes!" she exclaimed passionately. "But has God mentioned me?" He did not answer. "Abram!" she cried suddenly. "Let me speak while I can, before my woman's jealousy stops me! Hagar is yet young enough to give you a son. Take her. I give her to you as your second wife. Let the word of God come true through her, and perhaps because I have been unselfish and set myself aside, honor at least will come to me in place of the children I— *should* have had. . . ." Her voice broke up in violent tears of grief.

Abram was still for a long time, holding her gently in his arms. When she became a little calmer, he spoke slowly.

"It is true God has not mentioned you by name," he said at last. "Perhaps this is indeed His purpose . . . For how long can a man beget sons? I am old already and my vigor must soon leave me. . . . I will do as you say." As she gasped with pain he went on quickly, "But remember, for me you will always be the first and the dearest, for you see I did not set you aside for childlessness, nor ever suggest taking another wife. I have loved only you, and in this nothing will change."

Sarai drew away from him and went to her tent. She washed her face and changed into a pure white robe. Her own hair was nearly white now, and so pale was she that when she called Hagar before her, Hagar was shocked, for her mistress looked all gray in the black tent shadows, like a spirit.

"Hagar," said Sarai, her voice sounding hollow like someone speaking into a deep well. "Hear my command. You are to go to my husband and lie with him and be his wife. I have given you to him, so that the word of God can be fulfilled through you."

Hagar stared at her in absolute astonishment. Was such generosity possible? "Is this your true wish?" she asked at last in a low voice.

"It is my order," said Sarai.

Hagar, as the second wife of Abram, no longer served Sarai as before. Sarai chose another handmaiden from among her women, a shy, big-boned, awkward girl with a wide, flat face and rust-colored plaits twisted around her forehead, giving her a look of stupidity. Sarai suffered her clumsy service in scornful silence, never asking herself why she had chosen such an obviously unworthy replacement for the beautiful, intelligent Hagar. Some inner compulsion led her to make her own life as intolerable as possible, even in small ways.

Abram kept a scrupulous fairness in his division of himself between the two women, but Sarai thought she could detect a change in him—he seemed more youthful, his movements lighter and quicker, his laughter (never very usual with him) more frequent. Sometimes Sarai would hear him laughing with Hagar in his tent at night. The sound sent brutal spears of anguish through her body as she lay alone.

She watched Hagar secretly, hating herself for it.

While concealing even from herself the deepest hope of her heart, that Hagar, too, would be unable to bear, she could not control a certain ignoble lift of her spirits each day that Hagar's figure appeared unchanged.

But those days did not last long.

After a very few months, it became obvious to everyone that Hagar was with child. But Sarai was the first to know it, for her eye was sharpened for the least sign, and the first she detected was not Hagar's swelling womb but a new proud lift of her head, a new arrogance in her bearing. And when, in an effort to save Sarai pain, Abram told her himself, she merely turned away from him and said, "Why do you tell me what the world can see? She is as round as a ewe's rump already." Abram, shocked by Sarai's wholly uncharacteristic crudeness, left the tent, looking very serious.

One morning, Sarai's new handmaid dropped an earthenware jug of milk inside the tent, shattering it and splashing milk everywhere. Sarai flew into a rage and dismissed her. Then she went to Abram.

"Your new wife has turned lazy," she said. "Perhaps in Egypt, that land of licentiousness and idling, it is usual for a healthy woman scarcely into her fifth month to lie in her tent all day and be waited upon by her elders, but among our people it is not so."

"Do you wish her to serve you again?"

"Have you not noticed I have no handmaiden?"

"Take Hagar back into your tent, then. But"—he could not help adding—"treat her with care, and do not endanger my heir."

Hagar came back to serve Sarai as she was ordered, with some appearance at first of her old humility, but this did not deceive Sarai. Every movement of Hagar's body seemed a swagger of inner pride; every glance from those sly, slanted eyes filled Sarai with a sense of her own inferiority. She drove Hagar as she had never driven her, ordering her here and there, upbraiding her when she moved too slowly, commanding her to lift heavy objects, and scolding her like a child for insolence real or imagined. Hagar bore it as long as she could, but at last, when for the first time Sarai had so far lost control as to strike her across the face for merely looking askance at her, Hagar gave vent to her own hot temper.

"And why may I not look at you? I am your equal now, even though I serve you for my lord's sake! Is this your righteousness, to treat me so jealously? If you are as pious as they say, why has God cursed you for so many years and blessed me immediately?"

Sarai felt her scalp prickle with the onset of ungovernable rage. Her hand groped about of its own accord and found a length of rope. With an inarticulate cry, the old woman flew at the younger, swinging the rope about her shoulders with all the considerable strength that was still in her. Hagar, shielding her head and shutting her mouth tight, fled, with Sarai in pursuit, out of the tent and out of the camp, scattering the flock and leaving the herdboys gaping in astonishment.

Sarai chased her to the edge of the encampment and then stood, panting, watching with a satisfaction that must soon give way to shame Hagar's now ungainly figure running on and on along the dusty sheep track, her hands clutching her head. Then Sarai turned and walked heavily back, still breathing hard. The rope end dropped unnoticed into a rut.

Abram was waiting for her. He looked at her in wordless reproach.

"It is your fault," said Sarai sullenly. "You saw how she spited me, how she scorned me with her eyes, yet you said nothing. How was I expected to endure it?"

"It was you who offered her to me," Abram said.

"Do not remind me. I offered something beyond my strength. But if I was a fool, so were you to accept. When a woman does not understand herself, her husband must try to understand her better."

"God told me to accept."

"God! God! God!" shouted Sarai, suddenly raising both fists above her head. "God has caused this misery and dissension to fall on us! Why is He not more merciful? When have we ever disobeyed Him? If He really sees everything, He must see how unjustly I have been treated, and forgive me for my cruelty to that wretched woman! Oh, Abram," she sobbed suddenly, throwing herself upon him, "I am so ashamed!"

He gentled her. "My poor wife," he said quietly. "She will come back. All will be well. You will laugh again."

"Never, never." She wept exhaustedly. "There is no laughter left in me any more."

Several days passed, days of nightmarish terror for Sarai and sickening apprehension for Abram, who did indeed accept some part of the guilt for the situation. In truth, his fears were nearly all for the unborn child, but Sarai, seeing him so distraught, thought otherwise, and cried all the more.

When at last Hagar walked into the encampment, looking weary and unwashed and half starved, but with a new air of resignation and calm, both the old people rushed to her with open arms as if they had been her parents. Sarai attended her with her own hands, bathing her sore feet and bringing her warm camel's milk to drink. When Hagar was a little rested, Sarai humbled herself to say, "Forgive me for my wickedness. Some demon took hold of me."

Hagar looked at her but said nothing. Her eyes had a strange, feverish glitter. Sarai went on, almost timidly.

"Why did you come back? Weren't you afraid?"

"Yes, I was afraid. But I was persuaded to come."

"Persuaded? By whom?"

"By the God of Abram," she answered clearly.

Sarai fell back upon her heels. "He spoke to you—a woman?" she asked in a whisper.

"Not He Himself, but His messenger. He found me as I lay beside a well in the wilderness. I was dying, I think, for I had no strength to drink. And he asked me who I was and how I came there, and I told him I was running away from my mistress. And he said I should come back and submit myself to you."

Sarai was stunned. Never in all the years had God spoken to *her*. But perhaps it was just a tribesman or a shepherd, she thought. "Was that all?"

"No. But the rest was for me alone."

Hagar stood up then and began to busy herself about the tent, doing her work for Sarai as if nothing had happened. Sarai watched her in awe and amazement, for she seemed quite strong again, and genuinely humble as before she married Abram. No more insolent looks or arrogant gait . . . That night Hagar lay alone under the stars, but as the moon was about to set she saw Sarai standing beside her.

"Did his talk concern your child?" she asked.

"Yes."

"You would not be carrying a child if I had not brought it about," said Sarai. "I have a right to know."

After a long silence, Hagar spoke through the darkness. "He will be a wild man, as wild as I felt, out there alone and in terror. All men will be his enemies. But he will triumph over them all, because his seed shall found a great nation, and they shall remember what you did to me, and shall avenge me."

Sarai quailed inwardly at the clear ring of certainty in her voice.

"How? I shall die before they are born."

"I don't know or care. God heard my cry and answered it, and because of that I shall call my son Ishmael."

Sarai crept back to her tent and huddled there till first light, deeply afraid.

When Ishmael was born, Abram made a celebration. Sarai, summoning up all her resources, put jealousy and apprehension aside and joined in the merrymaking, taking care of Hagar personally and not failing to praise the baby, who was indeed a lovely, sturdy, well-made little boy, with smooth, olive-toned skin like his mother and a mass of curly black hair. Abram could not bear to be long out of sight of him, and for much of the night's revelry carried the baby everywhere with him in the crook of his arm.

Ishmael grew strong and healthy, and as wild as the desert wildcat. He was unbiddable save by his father, for whom he would have jumped down a well or tied himself behind an unbroken camel; as for his mother, it was enough that she told him to do something for him to do the opposite, and laugh at her when she tried to punish him.

And Sarai grew older still. All thoughts of children of her own had now left her, and a sort of peace came on her with the final loss of hope. She tried to look on Ishmael as her son, at least in part, but Hagar had no more children and was possessive. Sarai, ever conscious that she had wronged Hagar once, looked on this refusal to share the child as a fair punishment, and kept more and more to herself, trying to conquer her jealousy and live as good a life as she could, grateful to God for at least taking the edge off her bitterness.

When Ishmael was thirteen, something of the greatest possible importance happened. Abram came back from one of his sojourns in the hills and gathered all the men among his people together. But while this was being done, some of the herdsmen being at some distance and having to be fetched home, Abram took Hagar and Ishmael and Sarai into his tent.

He stood before them, so obviously in a state of the greatest agitation and excitement that the women exchanged glances. But it was the boy who could not contain himself, and asked, "Father, what's happened? Is it good news? Is it to do with me?"—for he was still the center of the world to himself. Abram took his curly head into his gnarled old hands and said, "My son, it is first to do with me, and then you, and then all those men who are gathering outside. God has put a hard duty on me, which will go hard with you too, but it is only a little part of a great matter and we must do it and smile at the pain. Pain is only of the present, but the sacred agreement God wishes to make with me is for the future, for many, many generations to follow us." But the boy heard only the word "pain" and said, "What pain, Father? What must I do?" and Abram said, "Follow me and set a brave example before the men, as I hope to set one before you."

Ishmael opened his mouth, but Abram went on, "This agreement, this holy, binding promise, is to be called a covenant between God and us, His chosen people. The sign of it we, the men, will wear on our bodies, on that part which is sacred to propagation. Today we will perform that act upon ourselves which will make us different from all other tribes, so that God may see and recognize us, and fulfill His word to give us His blessing forever, and the land He has promised to my descendants."

He laid his hands on the women's shoulders and looked at them both tenderly. "Go away from this place," he said, "and get water ready, and ointments, and strips of cloth." Sarai, completely bewildered, went at once, not looking back even when she heard Hagar cry out and come running after her.

"Sarai, what is to happen? My lord has set a piece of cork between the boy's teeth for him to bite on! What is he going to do to him that we may not see?"

"Do not ask. Do not think. Do as you were told."

"But he won't hurt him—his own son?"

"If God asked it of him," said Sarai grimly, "he would slaughter him like a sheep, or you, or me, or himself. Help me prepare the dressings."

After the mass circumcision, Ishmael recovered with all the resilience of adolescence, but for the old man it was a serious operation and his pain persisted a long time.

One shimmeringly hot day, just at noon when the sun's blows seemed to strike sparks from the rocks like a hammer upon red-hot metal, Abram, lying just inside his tent mouth, saw three men in white approaching across the plain. Their figures seemed to dissolve and reform in the heat waves that rose up from the baking ground, and Abram, watching them as they came, sat up suddenly. Sarai hurried to his side.

"What is the matter, why do you jerk your body like that?" she said anxiously.

"Some guests are coming," he said, staring into the deceptive heat haze.

"Who are they?" she asked, shading her eyes against the glare. "Do you know them?"

"I know who sent them," Abram said.

Soon the visitors came up to the tent, and to Sarai's dismay, her husband stood up from his bed and bowed low to them. Only she saw how his face twisted with pain as he did this; modestly hidden behind the tent flap, she stared resentfully at the strangers.

Abram was speaking to them in tones of reverence she had never heard him use before, even to visiting kings. He begged them to rest awhile under the shade of a thorn tree that stood by his tent, while he washed their feet and brought them food. They accepted, and reclined in the dusty shadow—a mere splash of shade in the white inferno of the plain—while Abram washed their feet with his own hands and then came hobbling back to the tent, his face alight with a look of eager joy that made Sarai bite back the sharp words she had been waiting to say. But when he ordered *three measures* of fine meal to be kneaded and made into cakes, it was all she could do to contain herself. Three full measures of meal for a mere three men! It was enough for all the principal men of their household. But she dared not argue.

Meanwhile, Abram hurried to the nearest herd and chose a fine young ox calf, which he gave to a servant with very careful orders about how it should be cooked. Then he fetched other delicacies—curd and milk—and gave these to the strangers. Sarai kept glancing at them from the dark tent. They looked quite ordinary—not like the emissaries of some great man—to merit such a welcome. . . . She pressed her lips together and blew out her nostrils in irritation.

At last the meal was eaten. The men had hardly spoken until now, which Sarai thought impolite, but now one of them suddenly asked, "Where is Sarah, your wife?"

Sarai's eyes opened as she heard this name. Her husband had told her, at the time of the circumcision, that God had ordered her name to be changed to Sarah. He had of course obeyed, but he seldom had occasion to say her name and she was not used to it yet—nor to calling him by his new name, Abraham. The meanings of these names were plain, but what God had meant by the change was not; for while "Sarai" meant "my princess," meaning the princess of just one man, "Sarah" meant princess in a more general sense; and Abraham meant "father of many." More immediately puzzling, however, was how these strangers knew her new name.

Abraham was pointing to the tent. Sarah cowered down to make sure she was well hidden, but she was avidly listening, for here was some mystery which concerned her. The stranger went on, "In a year from now, I shall come back this way, and by that time Sarah your wife shall have a son."

Sarah was not outraged, or staggered, or even surprised. It was the old story, the old prophecy, now proven nonsense by the years and by her body which, far from being fit for childbearing, was nearing its time to die. She turned her face away from the tent opening, but not as she once would have done—to weep—but with a cold and bitter chuckle.

The stranger's voice rose and reached her distinctly.

"Why is your wife laughing? Is she thinking to herself, 'How can I possibly have a baby at my age?' Is anything too hard for God? I tell you I shall certainly return when this season comes around again, and at that time, you shall see, Sarah shall have a son."

A strange pang of fear stung Sarah, so that she clutched her throat as if to stifle the laugh that had betrayed her. Yet how could it, when she hadn't laughed aloud? So great was her sudden fear that, against all the inhibitions that should have prevented her from speaking or showing herself before strangers, she ran to the tent opening and cried out, "I didn't! I didn't laugh!"

The three men had their backs to her and were so far away that she had to shout to make sure they would hear. Yet the answer, given in a quiet voice by one of them, seemed to be spoken almost beside her, "But you did."

Abraham did not come back from seeing them off until darkness had fallen, and Sarah was snappish with worry about him. But he brushed her aside quite brusquely when she tried to ask where he had been so long and whether he had not better be resting.

"This is no time to rest!" he exclaimed. "I have been in conversation with Him who sent those who have been with us—"

Sarah interrupted. "Are you saying truly that those were God's messengers?" she said.

"How did you not see it at once, woman? Did they not, in your hearing, repeat the prophecy?"

"It is an old promise," she said slowly, "broken beyond repair. I did not heed it."

"You did worse—you laughed at it. Were you not ashamed when they heard you? Do you doubt the word of God?"

"Am I rather to doubt my understanding of my own nature? There is no possibility of new life beginning in this old body."

"Sarah!" said Abraham, putting stern emphasis on the new name. "To refuse to accept God's words is a sin. What He's promised will be fulfilled. So say no more, but be glad that we are to be blessed at last. For myself . . . I have believed it from the first and never faltered."

Sarah could hardly control a bitter smile at this, remembering how little persuasion he had needed from her to accept Hagar—surely Ishmael was nothing if not the living proof of Abraham's doubt. But she lowered her head and said nothing.

Abraham now began to pace the floor of the tent agitatedly as he told her a piece of truly awesome news. God was so angry about the wicked practices going on in Sodom that He was about to destroy the whole town. "If it is a sin to doubt God," Abraham exclaimed distractedly, "how much worse is it to argue with Him? Yet I had to. Lot is my own brother's son! I pleaded with the Lord to spare the town for the sake of the few righteous men in it— though probably Lot is the only one, if indeed he too hasn't succumbed to the unnatural vices around him. . . ."

"What are they?" Sarah asked, irresistibly curious.

Abraham frowned at her. "Abominations too horrible to enter the imaginings of a pure woman," he growled. "God's holy method of procreation twisted and perverted

to yield unsanctified pleasures . . . Undoubtedly they deserve their fate. But still I hope God will show His mercy
to our kinsman. . . ."

Sarah's mind strayed to the girls who had accompa-
nied them into Egypt. They were grown women long ago,
and most of them had husbands, but two of them were still
unmarried. How could Lot have taken them to live in a
place of wickedness? All her frustrated motherliness went
out to them, and she found herself praying for their safety.

But that was a half-felt prayer compared to the way
she wept and wailed and held up her hands in supplication
when, two nights later, they watched from a mountainside
the fantastic spectacle of the destruction of Sodom. The
heavens lowered themselves in the shape of huge, red-
bellied clouds till they almost touched the tops of the
houses. From where the watchers stood, these clouds almost obscured the town, but suddenly they split asunder
with a hideous roaring crash; sparks and what looked like
lumps of red-hot stone shot upward. The very air of the
valley shivered with the explosion, and when the rolling
waves of smoke dispersed a little, the town could be seen
blazing, with rivers of fire flowing with a deadly slow de-
structive insistence through the streets. The houses were
crumbling, melting into it; and from far above, it seemed
to the horrified Sarah that she could actually see cracks ap-
pearing in the ground into which some houses toppled
whole. But by this time she was so stupefied by shock and
distress that she could not be sure how much was real and
how much her eyes were deceiving her.

The spectacle of destruction did not end till dawn.
The town was no more—not one block of stone stood on
another, not a living thing moved among the smoking
ruins. Even Abraham was afraid to go down and search for
Lot, fearing that God's wrath was not yet spent. It was not
until months later, when they had given him up, that they
heard rumors that he and his two youngest daughters were

living in a cave in the hills. . . . His wife was not there, and both the daughters were with child. Sarah was too shocked to think clearly; she assumed the wicked men of Sodom were responsible.

The whole incident brought about a great change in Sarah. Until that time, she had somehow half believed in Abraham's God, never having seen or spoken with Him herself; she took Him, as it were, for granted as a part of Abraham's life. But after witnessing the destruction of Sodom in all its magnificence and terror, God became utterly real to her, too. She had seen His word come true, the reality following hard upon the prophecy. And if *that*, then why not another?

She could not discuss it with her husband, for she now looked upon him with greater awe than ever as the confidant of this all-powerful and newly confirmed Being. Instead she talked to Hagar.

At first she hesitated. She and Hagar could unite when occasion demanded, but there was still bad blood between them. However, they had much in common, and, besides, Hagar was the only woman close to her—and this was definitely a womanly matter.

She began by telling her the story of the three strangers, who had come one day when Hagar and Ishmael were away from the settlement. Hagar listened attentively, and asked for descriptions of the men, which Sarah found hard to give; but when she said that one man had spoken to her from a distance, and yet in a low, clear voice as if standing beside her, Hagar's dark face lit up and she exclaimed, "Yes! That is how it was with me, too, in the wilderness! The angel stood quite far from me, yet his voice came from close by."

"Then you think these, too, were angels?" asked Sarah in a hushed voice.

Hagar stared at her inscrutably. "What promise did they make you?"

Sarah, mumbling due to sudden deep embarrassment, said, "That a son would be born to me. Of course I know it sounds foolish."

After a long silence Hagar released a held breath with a sound like a gasp of pain. "God's word is true," she said.

"Then—then you think it will happen?" Sarah asked with a strange humility.

Hagar jumped up. She seemed agitated, standing over Sarah with clenched fists and flaring eyes. "How can I know?" she asked sharply. "All these years you have lived with Abraham and not conceived. . . . To me it was no surprise. There is more in these matters than piety and godliness! What do you desert women know of love? In Egypt I was taught the arts of pleasing a man. All these years you did no more than stretch your beauty upon the ground and wait for Abraham's seed to bring life into you, as the brute earth waits for the sower! Look at me! I have not half your portion of beauty, yet I conceived the very night Abraham first lay with me! Think, Sarah, my mistress and fellow wife—think back to Egypt. Think of the bathing and the perfumes, think of the soft scented garments that changed the way your body moved within them and of the jewelry that weighed down your wrists and neck and brought men's eyes upon you with their soft, beckoning jingle. You were different then! If my father, the Pharaoh, had had his will of you, you would have discovered how to conceive, for in his palace you were no mere furrow in the ground, nor were you filled with false notions of modesty and righteousness. You were a woman." She threw back her still-black head and laughed wildly. "To think! You have lived through all these many years—and have been a woman but three days in all of them, and never for your husband, but only as the chaste concubine of a foreign tyrant!"

In past times, Sarah would have flown at Hagar in blind fury at these outrages. But her age, and the strange terrors of the past months, had quenched the fires of her temper. Now she simply stared at Hagar in a sort of silent agony, and then turned and fled from her, running from the encampment as Hagar had once run from her anger.

Late at night she returned. No angel had come to comfort her as she lay out upon the plain, yet her weeping had stopped by itself and a strange resolution had come to her. The anguish of thinking that Hagar might have spoken a sort of truth had given way to determination. Old she was; yet God had promised that she might yet give birth. If that were true, then perhaps it was not too late to give and get pleasure—God could not give her the child without the means to get it. Her son, if there were to be a son, must not be conceived in passivity and patience, but in laughter and joy and rapture.

The encampment slept. But within her own tent, Sarah lit a lamp and called Hagar to her.

She came, blinking in astonishment, for Sarah stood before her naked.

"Wash and prepare me," Sarah said, "after the manner of Egypt. My heart is light and I feel again a whisper of young womanliness in my body. Make me desirable, for God has made me a promise that tonight must see fulfilled."

The now very large numbers of people in Abraham's household had always regarded God as a more or less legendary being whose mouthpiece, Abraham, was actually the god figure for ordinary men such as themselves. God was not real to them, though they claimed belief in Him. There had been nothing to them miraculous about the birth of Ishmael, and even the destruction of Sodom—which they had not personally seen—could have been a natural catastrophe. They were superstitious enough to say their prayers and follow the rituals Abraham prescribed;

but it was not until the incredulous household learned that their old mistress was with child that they fell on their faces as one man and offered genuine and heartfelt worship to an all-powerful and miraculous deity.

They crept up to touch Sarah's robe or even her tent, to ask for her blessing and to bring their children to her to receive her protection from the evil eye. And what they saw when they came close to her amazed and awed them still more. For Sarah had about her a look of restored youth. Perhaps it was an illusion; but as her figure burgeoned, throwing her weight backward, her stooped shoulders straightened, her movements lost their fumbling, decrepit quality; her eyes were bright, and her skin regained some of its bloom and smoothness as her face filled out with the flesh of good rich food which, suddenly, she relished again.

She dressed quite differently, too—discarding the rusty old black garments of an aged Bedouin and donning a kaftan of rich color and texture, brilliantly embroidered, which she had been given in her youth by the Pharaoh. She did no work—Abraham forbade it—but reclined outside her tent during the cooler hours of the day, receiving the homage of her people and the slavish service of her handmaidens.

But the greatest change was her laughter. She laughed at small things, or at nothing at all—nothing, that is, that was happening outside her; yet some secret thought of her own would bring her such inner happiness and gaiety of heart that she would laugh aloud at it, not caring who heard. People passing would laugh with her, and go on about their work feeling light-spirited and full of joy. It was a world in which all wonders were possible; they rested content in the shadow of these two old people, the favored of a mighty and, at last, entirely convincing God.

When Sarah's time came, she demanded that Hagar and none other should be her midwife. Hagar performed her office with an expressionless face and infinite care, and then carried the lustily bawling boy child out to Abraham wrapped in a spotless lamb's pelt. Abraham, radiant with joy and with the glow of rewarded faith seeming to lend his aged face a sort of incandescence, took the baby reverently in his arms and carried it to his own altar, where he laid it, still crying. A vast crowd of people gathered around in awed silence and watched while Abraham prayed, prostrate with his beard and forelock touching the sand.

Then he stood up and said, "His name shall be Isaac" —and all the people sighed with pleasure, because this name means "He laughs," and it reminded them of their own and Sarah's happiness.

Isaac was a very different child from Ishmael. Where Ishmael had been wild and headstrong from the first, Isaac was gentle, obedient, and charming. He was the joy of his parents' hearts; far more than the natural love a mother and father feel for a son was lavished on Isaac because of the years they had longed for him, and also because they knew him to be God's personal gift to them, a reward for their years of service to Him. When Sarah feasted her eyes upon her beloved child, she was often stricken with pangs of conscience because her life had not been perfect enough truly to deserve such an unmixed blessing.

But Sarah's imperfections were still to find her out.

When Isaac was two years old, Sarah knew that her time of miraculous second youth was over. Her body once more had the appearance of extreme age, and, in tears, she told Abraham that the boy must be weaned.

Abraham laughed away her tears. "Our son is half a man already!" he said robustly. "Why do you weep, foolish mother of my son? Do you wish him to be a baby forever? Be glad that he is growing toward manhood—who knows, you may yet be a grandmother before you die!"

He hurried off then to arrange a great feast to celebrate this first milestone in Isaac's life. All his people put on their finest clothes; quantities of good meat were prepared, and the best wine, and rich cakes enough for a multitude. Hagar watched the preparations narrowly. No such feast had been held for the weaning of Ishmael, but this was only part of what hurt her heart. Isaac was not stronger or better-looking than her own son, but already he showed a different and more attractive nature. Isaac was the darling of the settlement, and at the same time an object of reverence, while Ishmael, now a harum-scarum lad of seventeen, was more and more frowned on or ignored.

Another matter troubled her. Her son was of course the elder, and so should be Abraham's primary heir; yet Sarah was the first wife—could she perhaps claim priority for her son? Hagar had always considered herself a legitimate wife of Abraham; but something in the way Sarah had looked at her and spoken to her since Isaac's birth made her suspect that Sarah might regard her as a concubine, whose son could not inherit except such a portion as his father chose to allot him out of kindness.

Ishmael was, for all his brashness, not insensitive. He was fully aware of the dislike he caused, and of his fall from favor since the advent of Isaac. But what cut him most deeply was that his adored father seemed as besotted with the newcomer as everybody else was. While still treating Ishmael with kindness, he no longer spent much time talking to and teaching him, or even scolding him, but let him go his own way while he played with his new son. As a result Ishmael felt a passion of jealousy that hardly ever left him, and his behavior grew more outlandish.

At first he refused to attend the feast, but when Hagar told him that his father would be insulted, he sullenly strolled into the midst of it, throwing sneering looks about him from under his heavy black eyebrows, not speaking to anyone or doing anything to help. Once or twice, when he dared, he would kick over a skin of wine with his foot and then stand and watch while the red stain spread over the ground before swaggering insolently away. But within him his heart burned with misery as he watched his father tossing his half brother into the air, laughing into his face with pride.

It was Sarah who noticed him at last, and called him over to her.

"Well, Ishmael," she said kindly. "Why are you not eating? You are hungry enough as a rule. Come, you mustn't scowl, or Isaac will be more handsome than you. See how all the world laughs for my son! Let me see you laugh, too, or I shall think you don't love him as a brother must."

"I love him," said Ishmael sourly. "I love him all right, as an elder brother loves a younger. Let him look to it that he loves me, and pays me respect, because I am my father's heir and he comes second to me. That is something we must soon teach him. It is a pity he is weaned," he went on recklessly, ignoring the stiffening look of anger in Sarah's face, "for a child should draw in such knowledge of his place with his mother's milk. Otherwise, with all this fuss which you are making of him, he might get a false impression and think himself the heir instead of me."

Sarah felt all the old violent rage flood through her as if repentance had never touched her mind. But this time she controlled it. Sitting, apparently calm, dignified, and sedate, she merely looked at Ishmael, and disguised the trembling of her hands by picking up Isaac and fondling him.

"These matters are not for women or boys to dispute," she said quietly. "They are decisions for him who is the father of you both." And she turned away from him.

But her anger devoured all her pleasure in the feast,

and that night, very late when it was all over and she and Abraham were standing in their tent looking down upon their sleeping child, Sarah suddenly said, "She is not, and never was, your true wife. I was destined for that honor before I was born, and you swore to me when you agreed to take her that I would always come before her and have pride of place."

"What is this about?" Abraham asked in alarm. "More women's folly? Hagar is my second wife and her son is my true son. Perhaps I have neglected him since this little one came. . . . But he is mine and I love him, for all his headstrong, unruly manners."

"He is worse than headstrong!" Sarah exclaimed, turning to him and grasping his sleeves. "He is not worthy to be your heir! All her wildness and rebelliousness are in him. She is not of our people! And if God did not wish His covenant with you to be fulfilled through *my* son, why did He intervene, against all that was natural, to give Isaac to me?" Abraham drew away from her, gazing at her.

"Woman, what are you about? Would you invite more remorse upon yourself, as when you drove her out before?"

"That was something else. She was pregnant and helpless then and I did very wrong. I acted from personal jealousy. But it is no sin to protect the heritage of one's son, especially one so obviously blessed as my Isaac is. Look at him, my lord! Is he not in every way a properer child than Ishmael? He has no vice in him, no cruelty, no bitterness of heart such as the other has shown me only tonight!" And she told him of the incident at the feast when Ishmael had mocked at Isaac.

Abraham said nothing, but his spirit sank so low with apprehension and grief that he couldn't move and his head hung down.

"If you let Ishmael remain, there will be endless trouble between those two," Sarah was saying. "Already I have seen Ishmael shooting arrows at the little one . . . Oh, it was only in play, but I saw his face as he shot them—it was full of hatred. One day, who knows?—the arrows might be real."

Without moving, Abraham, in a broken voice, said, "What shall be done then?"

"Send her away," said Sarah. "And the boy with her. She was a slave at her own wish. Such a one can never be a true wife. Give her food and water and let her return to her own people."

Abraham's shoulders rose and fell in a single sob. "I cannot do it! I love him. And God has promised that I shall father a nation through him also."

"That prophecy was never made to *you*. We have only Hagar's word. But it may be true. . . ." She shrugged. "If so, God will preserve him. Our concern must be with Isaac, whom God has entrusted to us." And when Abraham still trembled and shook his head helplessly, she gave way completely to her weakness and, leaning toward him, whispered, "For whom did God work a miracle, Hagar or me? Whose child is the doing of God? For I tell you, husband, as you and Lot could not graze your flocks upon one mountainside, so Hagar and I cannot raise our sons in one tent. It is she or I, her son or mine. Choose."

Abraham stared at her with heartbreak in his face.

"Are you really a good woman?" he asked suddenly, as if to himself.

She shrank back, appalled.

"Leave me," he went on. "I will ask the Lord what His wishes are. What He orders me to do, that I will do, whatever the consequences."

Sarah lay awake all night, fighting her last great inner battle. By dawn, her better part had won, and she rose to go to Abraham and tell him that Hagar and Ishmael might stay. But even as she lifted the flap of her tent, she stiffened at the tableau in front of her.

Abraham, looking very old and exhausted, his face harrowed and his hands trembling, was in the act of lifting onto the shoulder of Hagar an earthenware bottle of water. Hagar stood before him, motionless. Ishmael stood beside her. He was nearly as tall as she; he had his arm around her shoulder protectively, and his other fist was clenched.

Even as Sarah looked, the first rays of sunrise burst over the horizon, touching first the three figures and a moment later the eyes of Sarah, behind them. The shaft, cutting through the clear air, half blinded her, and its effect on the scene she was looking at was, for just a moment, to coat the bodies of her husband and her rivals with blood.

At that second, Ishmael turned, attracted by Sarah's sudden convulsive movement, and saw her. His young face was set in lines of fury, bewilderment, and hatred. His mouth opened and his clenched fist half lifted; with his black, twisted brows and agonized eyes he had the look of a devil about to spring upon her.

But Abraham put his hand on the boy's shoulder and spoke to him quietly; the moment of menace passed, and the boy, taking the jar of water and the bundle of their possessions from his mother with a new and unwonted manliness, led her away.

Abraham and Sarah, standing separately, watched while the two banished members of their lives walked— Hagar slowly as if aged by shock, Ishmael with grim defiance—away across the plain, heading south.

They watched them out of sight. Then Abraham cast at Sarah a long look of unendurable pain and reproach before turning back into his tent where Isaac still lay sleeping.

Eleven years passed.

Relations between the patriarch and his wife remained strained for some time, but gradually the boy Isaac reunited them. He grew daily more wonderful in their eyes. "It would have been enough, had God given us just any son," Sarah exulted once. "But this boy shows in every way that God's hand placed him in my womb. I can all but see His finger marks still."

As she grew yet older, Sarah's whole world was in Isaac; indeed she clung almost feverishly to life long after her beauty had disintegrated and her strength departed, simply to stay near him in the flesh and have another day, and another, in his company. Her rapturous laughter when he was near her was the last remaining trace of her lost, miraculous youth.

The last day of her life began like any other. She rose early to catch the coolness of dawn, and prepared the usual simple breakfast of curd and flat bread and olives for Abraham and Isaac. She noticed that her husband and son had got up even earlier, but supposing that they had had some business with the herdsmen, who left for the pastures before dawn, she set out the meal when it was ready, expecting them every moment to return.

When they did not come, she wasn't alarmed. It happened sometimes that they were gone for a whole day, visiting neighboring tribes, or, in Isaac's case, out with the flocks learning from Abraham or his stewards the matters he needed to know. Abraham would often tell Sarah, with intense pride, how quick the boy was. "Were I to die tomorrow," he said, "Isaac could take over from me, young as he is."

Sarah, with the placidity of her great age, grunted to herself and laboriously sat down on the ground to wait for them. The sun crept up, and the sullen heat of noon settled over the tents. They did not come. Sarah's palsied head dropped lower and lower till her chin sank in sleep upon her chest.

God sent her a sweet dream of her youth: she saw herself and Hagar together—righteous and modest, yet full of laughter, and with the warm spring tide of sensuality flowing through her; she could taste again the ripe fruits and smell the musky perfumes of Egypt. When she was suddenly awakened, she found her wrinkled, fleshless arm half raised to let her admire the heavy gold bangles she had dreamt were upon it.

She started and looked around, wondering what had wakened her. Then she saw the man Eliezer at her feet.

He was her husband's chief steward. Before the birth of Ishmael, Abraham had appointed him his heir, having no direct descendant. Now he raised his face from the dust and stared at Sarah with an unreadable expression; his face was marked with sweat and dust, and his eyes glowed, hard and glazed. His breath gusted out, from desperate running; his sinewy arms, holding up his body from the ground, trembled and ran with sweat.

"Mistress—" he got out at last.

"Eliezer?"

"I have come—I have run—I have run all the way from Moriah."

"Moriah?" she asked, half asleep still and bewildered.

"It was still dark when the master woke me and told me to go with him and your son. . . . We mounted asses and rode till we came to the mountains. . . . My lord said we were going to offer up a sacrifice, but we took no lamb or calf for the offering, only a bundle of wood which he had prepared. I and the other steward were left at the foot of the mountain, and the master said he and your son would return after the sacrifice . . . they climbed up alone, with the boy carrying the wood, and my master the fire and the knife . . . we thought it strange, for where in those barren hills would a fit creature for the sacrifice be found? It was strange . . . and my lord was strange . . . so silent . . . as he gave us our orders, it seemed to us he wept. . . . And then they went upward, and we watched, and—and—and—oh, mistress! We beheld a deed so terrible that I cannot tell it to you!"

Sarah, filled already by a great, unspecified fear, leaned toward him and grasped his garment in one hand.

"Speak—"

Eliezer fell on his face again in the dust, but Sarah, with surprising strength, caught him now by the hair and dragged up his head.

"Speak!"

His hard eyes fixed themselves on her out of a mask of sweat blackened dust.

"Halfway up the mountain," he whispered, "we saw them halt. The old lord built an altar of stones while the boy watched. Then your husband turned suddenly—pulled the boy's arms behind him and bound them. Then he took him up and laid him on the altar."

Sarah screamed.

The man continued as if nothing had happened.

"He piled the faggots around him and then drew out his knife. He laid his hand upon the boy's face, pressing it backward so his throat might be stretched . . . I could watch no more! I cried out with terror and ran to tell you. But scream as you will, mistress"—for Sarah was beside herself now and no longer heard him for her own shrieks—"your husband has slain his last heir. The smoke of that sweet body is rising even now to your cruel God whom I worship no more . . . for He should have struck down your lord before He allowed such a sacrifice."

The encampment had wakened from its noontime stupor, and the clamor of its awakening rose up behind Sarah's desperate cries. Men's and women's voices, children's frightened outbursts, the bleating of the startled herds, and then the thudding of many feet as people came running.

But by the time they arrived and stood, crowded in horrified awe and silence around Sarah's tent, her screams had stopped. She sat for a moment, poised like an old bundle of rags which has momentarily been stood on end, and then her figure seemed to shrink and sag. It fell over sideways, quite slowly. Only the little spurts of dust it pushed up when it landed showed that there was anything solid inside the rusty black cloth.

Eliezer had told his tale till even his garrulous tongue was silenced by too much repetition and embellishment by the time the welcome cool of sunset came and people drifted back to their tents. Women had wept, and their tears evaporated; men had moaned and offered up prayers which seemed to hover in the hot, heavy air, for they doubted God again, and a prayer offered without faith does not rise.

Sarah's handmaidens had carried her—a light burden for two of them—into her tent and were tending her, but with the flap open so that they might not be cut off from the tumbling waves of horror, gossip, and speculation that were washing over the whole encampment. In appalled whispers they exchanged comments over the unconscious body of their mistress.

"It's a wonder the shock didn't kill her at once."

"She can't live long. Look at her face! She has the look of a corpse already."

"What when the old lord comes? How could he have told her?"

"Better she should never wake. Better for him that he die at her side tonight."

They did not touch upon the act at the core of it all, only upon the result, the impact upon the principals.

"It is a judgment upon them for their treatment of the other mistress."

"I cared little for Ishmael, but he was a true heir."

"Ah, but the boy! The sweet one, the darling!"

Both women began to rock and wail with genuine personal grief.

The sun was sinking. Sarah had not stirred. Suddenly a cry went up from the lookout, stationed beyond the farthest tents.

"They approach! They come! Aaaiiii!" His cry ended with a long-drawn, wild scream, the scream of a man stricken with terror and bewilderment.

The women left Sarah instantly and rushed outside. Clouds of dust were rising from the new surge of curious feet, and for a few moments they could not see the cause of the cry. People were running, pointing, calling out. A figure ran through the dust toward them.

"He lives, he lives! They are coming!"

At that, the women joined a great crowd of Abraham's people who were pushing and jostling down the little slope toward the plain. Shouts went up; the dust grew thicker than ever. But abruptly the crowd made way and Abraham loomed through the gritty dusk like an aged specter, pulling his weary body forward with his stick; and behind him came Isaac, travel-stained but clearly no ghost, looking around him in amazement as the shouting died down and people reached out to touch him in verification and wonder as he passed.

When Abraham saw Sarah's handmaidens, he stopped.

"What is the matter here, what is going on?" he asked testily.

They stared at him speechlessly.

"Speak, can't you? Where is my wife?"

"Ill, my lord," one of them managed to whisper at last. "She lies in her tent."

"Ill?" barked Abraham. "With what is she ill?"

"The news, master—"

"What news do you mean? Speak clearly."

But the woman, covering her head, turned and fled into the crowd.

Abraham did not wait to ask more, but hurried as fast as possible to Sarah's tent. It was dark and dusty inside, and there was a strange smell—perhaps no more than an atmosphere—which made the old man stop short and cry out. He and Isaac sank to their knees beside the rough pallet on the ground where Sarah lay.

As his hand, trembling with age, weariness, and sorrow, touched her, Sarah's eyes opened. Abraham could just see the reflection of a little light gleaming on the crescents of moisture in the heavy gloom.

"Wife," he whispered, leaning over her.

"Why—?"

It was the faintest breath of sound from the dying lips.

With a sensation as of a blow to the heart, Abraham understood.

"Look, beloved. He lives. It was only God's final test of my faith—He stopped me. He stopped my hand! Sarah—"

Sarah's eyes did not move. Only her lips parted for the last time. The very weakness of her voice made the reproach more poignant.

"You meant to do it."

Fumblingly, Abraham pushed the boy into his mother's line of vision. Isaac, all but overcome by the events of this most terrible day of his life, quite unable to realize that his mother was on the verge of death, flung himself upon her breast like a child. He slid his arms under her shoulders and lifted the frail but suddenly heavy body till he clasped it awkwardly to his young chest. He kissed her face, feeling the papery wrinkles under his lips, calling to her as if across a growing distance, "Mother—*Mother!*"

Did she know him? Did her hand reach up in that last, dim moment of consciousness, to touch his back? He was never sure. But he felt the life go out of her. He laid her down, the way one lays down a baby, his hand supporting her head, and drew in his breath in one raw, jagged sob.

His father was prostrate on the ground at her side.

The boy stood up and looked down on them both. He checked his tears. He had to step over his father to leave the tent.

Outside he faced the silent crowd, pressing in through the sudden desert darkness.

"She is dead," he said clearly.

They made a path for him. No one tried to touch him now. He didn't see them as he passed through them.

He walked till he was out of the dust, until the moon and stars hung above him, clean and clear. As a child he had always regarded the moon as the eye of God. Now it was crooked and half closed. Isaac sat down with his arms around his raised knees and stared up at it. He forced himself to live again through that timeless moment of horror and fear as his father's hand had pushed back his chin and he had, by casting down his eyes, been able to see the handle of the knife poised for an eternity against his stretched throat. As he thought of it, the tendons there vibrated like harp strings.

He meant to do it. . . .

His own father!

Was that why the eye was half closed? To prevent his reading its secret?

But he knew it already. You loved God, or you loved people. To do both, when God could demand *this*. . . .

It was a mystery too deep for him. He laid his head on his knees and wept for his mother.

Two

———◆———

Rebecca

*A*s *Issac grew* up his father and all about him saw how gravely that fatal day in his boyhood had affected him. His relationship with Abraham was never the same. He treated his father with the utmost respect and never, by so much as a single word, reproached him for his intention on the Mount of Moriah or for Sarah's terrible death; but Abraham knew without words that the boy—his heart's most precious treasure—was divided from him by a gulf nothing could bridge.

But Isaac did not grow bitter. He only grew more gentle, more quiet; his grief and moral perplexity expressed itself in kindness to the old and patience with the young. He seldom raised his voice, and never lost his temper. No one ever saw him perform a violent act. Even necessary violence, like the slaughter of animals, he avoided, delegating these tasks to his stewards. In one thing only he went against his father's commands: he refused to sacrifice live animals on God's altar. Abraham, feeling for once in his life unable to meet the situation, did not insist. He himself had no taste for sacrifice any more. Sacrifices had to be made, of course; but he appointed Eliezer, still his chief steward, to do this duty, saying by way of excuse that his old hand had no longer the strength to wield the knife. And this was true.

One day Isaac led his flocks far out across the desert,

and when he returned at evening and was sitting with his father as duty demanded, but silently brooding as usual, he suddenly said, "Father, what is that well on the way to Shur? Somehow I have never found it before."

"Between Kadesh and Bered?" asked his father slowly. Isaac nodded. "That we call Be'er-Lehai-Ro-i, the well of the Living One Who Sees Me."

"Why?"

The old man hesitated, but, after all, what more harm could be done? Lies could not help to bring his son closer to him.

"My second wife, Hagar, named it thus." And he told Isaac the story of Hagar and Ishmael in full for the first time, keeping nothing back.

Isaac made no comment, except to ask, "And where are they now, my brother Ishmael and his mother?" And Abraham said that they had gone south, he did not know exactly where, but that he had heard that Ishmael had married a girl from among his mother's people and she had born him several sons. "And are they happy? Is Hagar happy?" Isaac asked. But Abraham only shrugged and shook his head.

The thought of Ishmael being married, and a father, did not trouble Isaac, who had no desire to marry. On the contrary, he wished to keep himself even from the danger of loving anyone. But it troubled Abraham greatly. For here they were, living in the land of the Canaanites—a foreign tribe, despite their long residence among them. Their own people were mainly the descendants of the Eyptians given to Abraham by the Pharaoh long ago, or the results of intermarriage between them and the Canaanites. There was not one woman of Abraham's own people whom he could give to Isaac as a wife, and Abraham was determined that his son should marry a girl of his own race. And it was time, for Isaac was already past his first youth.

So one day Abraham called Eliezer to him in his tent.

Eliezer was quite an elderly man now, and had been Abraham's chief steward for so long that he could guess his wishes and anticipate his orders almost before he found words for them in his trembling old voice. But on this occasion, Eliezer found his old master could still astonish him.

"Eliezer, you have command over all that is mine. Have I still command over you?"

The steward bowed low.

"I have now a mission for you which will take you far away, back to the country from which, long ago, I brought my young wife and a few of our tribesmen, and Lot, my brother's son, and his family. I left many of my kinsmen behind, where no doubt they still are, with their descendants. It is to that distant place that you must go, and there, from among my own people, choose a wife for my son."

Eliezer gazed at the old man anxiously. Here was a task! To choose the woman who would be the mother of Isaac's children, through whom the great prophecies would be fulfilled! Eliezer was a man who knew his duty, but this responsibility was one he would infinitely have preferred to avoid if he could. But there was no question of that. He was the proper person for the assignment, and he would have to do his best.

Abraham then made Eliezer put his hand under his shriveled thigh, as was the custom, and swear an oath of the greatest solemnity that he would not choose a wife for Isaac from among the daughters of the Canaanites, no matter what happened.

"What if the woman I choose is unwilling to leave her family and follow me back into this land, which is strange to her?" Eliezer asked, "Shall I, in that case, take your son back to Ur?"

Abraham sat up with as much sharpness as his old body was capable of, pressing Eliezer's imprisoned hand hard upon the ground as he did so. "Whatever you do, don't take him back there!" he cried. "God, who took me from my father's house and from the land of my birth, promised that my seed would inherit *this* land. So undoubtedly God will guide you to the right woman. If she doesn't agree to come back here, it can only be because you have chosen wrongly, for God will make sure that the right one will come. Now, be gone quickly about this business. I'm getting very old. These things must be accomplished, and my grandchildren delivered into the world, before I can die in peace."

Eliezer made his preparations with great care. He chose ten camels and loaded them with beautiful presents from his master's store of treasure and wealth—all sorts of delicate clothing, and jewels, and gold, and the finest ornaments.

At last he was ready and set out across the fields, following, though he did not know it, the very track that Abraham had beaten out with his flocks all those years ago, coming down toward Egypt.

The journey was a long one, but Eliezer's mind was so occupied with heavy thoughts of his responsibility that it seemed a remarkably short time before he saw ahead of him, glowing in the evening light, the town of Padan-Aram of the Two Rivers. He had not rested much on the way, and the beasts and their attendants were tired and very thirsty. There was a well outside the walls of the city, and when they smelled the water the weary animals knelt down beside it and refused to go on. Eliezer's servants went ahead to draw some water but Eliezer stopped them.

"Wait," he said.

An idea had come to him. Going between two of the kneeling camels, where he could not be seen, he knelt down himself, with his head resting against one of the warm, strong-smelling camel blankets, and prayed.

"O Lord God of my master Abraham, help me in my time of need, and show kindness to my master. I see the women of the city coming now through the gates, in the evening coolness, to fill their vessels at the well. Perhaps the very girl I should choose for Isaac is one of them—but how shall I know her if You do not give me a sign? So let it be like this: I shall ask several of these young women for a drink, and the one who gives it to me, and even offers to draw water for my camels, she shall be the one You have appointed."

Then he stood up and looked across the camels' backs.

A group of girls was approaching. They were a charming sight, and Eliezer, old as he was, delighted to watch their graceful, swaying movements, the straight carriage of their bodies, and the natural poise of their heads on each of which rested a heavy earthenware pitcher. They were veiled, but their eyes and the skins of their foreheads and arms glowed in the warm reddish light of the setting sun which glanced off the golden sand. Their laughter, and the sweet singing of one of them, splashed the air around them like the sound of sheep bells ringing beside a fountain.

As they came nearer, Eliezer scanned their faces anxiously. It was hard to distinguish one from another; each moved smoothly, each kept her eyes modestly lowered when she noticed the presence of a strange man. As they took the pitchers from their heads and began to draw water to fill them, Eliezer moved until he stood beside them.

One girl was bending close to him. Her veil had been caught by some roughness on the base of the pitcher and been pulled a little askew, revealing her tumbling black hair which fell over her shoulder, and the top of her rounded cheek as she half turned to glance shyly up at him. Eliezer noticed her eyes—huge, almond-shaped, deep black, and shining—before the thick lashes, like the fringe on a piece of drapery, dropped over them.

He waited until she had filled her pitcher and lifted it

to her shoulder, and then said, "I am very thirsty. Will you give me a little water?"

The girl looked at him for a moment, her eyes wide open, and he looked back at her. How easily, he thought later, she might have mistaken that straight, bold look and turned from him, her modesty affronted. But she didn't. Instead she painfully lifted the heavy jar off her shoulder and said, in a voice of the utmost gentleness and sweetness, "Drink, my lord."

He did not help her to hold it, but leaned forward, and she carefully leveled the pitcher to his mouth and tilted it till a trickle of ice-cold water flowed into his mouth. It tasted so good to him that he could not stop drinking, although he knew how her fragile arm must be aching with the weight of the pitcher held at that awkward angle. He drank and drank, and at last he was satisfied and stepped back. A light beading of perspiration had sprung out upon her high, dusky forehead.

"I have tired you, my girl," said the old steward.

"No! Let me now draw enough water for your camels."

Eliezer's heart gave a leap of joy. God had heard him, and here, before his eyes, stood the very girl he had come to seek. There could be no error, for the other girls were laughing at her for giving herself so much extra work— clearly none of them would have volunteered to water so many thirsty beasts, who between them drank and drank until the poor child had no strength to draw more for them. Then at last Eliezer felt free to take the bucket gently from her hands, which trembled with tiredness, and finish the task while she rested herself, sitting on the well's edge. She was alone now; her companions had all left her to go home; and she had amply fulfilled her offer, so that she might have left, too—it would have been only fitting for her to do so, instead of staying there, alone in the twilight with strangers—yet she sat on, watching him without shame, as if waiting for him to tell her what she must do next.

"God's hand is on her," thought Eliezer exultantly. "And I am His messenger!" He glanced at her slim, swathed figure as she sat there, her hands limp in her lap. From that virginal body would come the great race of men who would people the desert. Ah, if only he were free to give her a hint of her destiny! But it would be too much for her to bear.

When the camels had at last drunk their fill, and the last blood-red rim of the sun was disappearing in a welter of brilliant dust clouds, Eliezer went to one of the brightly colored woolen saddlebags and took out a small, heavy packet. He went straight to the girl and, lifting one hand, slipped onto her finger a thick gold ring. Even while she was staring in amazement at this, he hung a gold bracelet on each of her slender arms.

She stared up at him wordlessly, with the dull gold of the ornaments faintly gleaming on her wrists.

"What are you called?" Eliezer asked her.

"Rebecca."

"Whose daughter are you?"

"I am the daughter of Bethuel, son of Milcah, the wife of Nahor."

Eliezer caught his breath. This much of a miracle he had not expected, for Nahor was none other than Abraham's own brother, so that this girl was a close kin to his master.

"Is there room for us to lodge in your father's house?"

"There is room, and we have plenty of fodder for your camels."

"Go, then. Leave your pitcher here, and run and tell your mother that we are coming."

The moment she was gone, Eliezer threw himself onto the ground with his face in the dust and thanked God with all his heart. Then he stood up, gathered his servants together, and led them slowly toward the city gates.

Meanwhile Rebecca ran home, her heart beating with a strange mixture of terror and excitement. The bracelets felt like heavy weights, drawing her wrists toward the ground, and the ring was so thick she could not press her fingers together on either side of it. It was the first jewelry she had ever worn. The thought of the stranger's eyes and the touch of his alien fingers on her hands made her tremble. What would her brother Laban say to her for allowing herself to be thus handled, for accepting these rich, compromising gifts? What had possessed her to do so? It was completely against all her upbringing, and yet . . . remembering it, she felt she had had no choice. But how could the men of her family be expected to understand the strange feeling of helplessness which had held her prisoner there by the well? They might beat her and then go down and kill the bold intruder.

So she decided to speak first to her mother and let her decide what to do. Running into the part of the house where the women did the cooking and preparing of food, she flung herself on the ground at her mother's knees and wordlessly thrust out her arms. Her garments fell back, and the lamplight lit up the gold like bangles of fire.

Her mother stared for a moment, then seized upon the jewelry, smoothing it with her blunt, workworn fingers.

"Where did you get these?" she asked her daughter sharply.

"A man—an old man—a stranger put them on me," Rebecca gasped. "Truly, Mother, I don't know why! It must have been a reward because I gave him and his camels water."

"How many camels?" at once asked the mother, her eyes glistening.

"Many," said Rebecca, who could not count. "As many as my hand has fingers."

"All laden?"

"I think so—"

"You did well to water them, Rebecca," said her mother decidedly. "Come with me. We will tell your brother."

"You will not let him harm the stranger—or—or me?"

Her mother heaved her large bulk up from the floor by clutching her daughter's arm, and then kept her hand clasped around the cold, precious band as she led her to the men's quarters.

"No one will be harmed, not if I know your brother," she said.

Laban took one look at the gold as his mother wordlessly held it out to him, careless of the wrists that it encircled. He flashed a hard, questioning look at his sister, and Rebecca tremblingly explained all that had happened.

Without speaking, Laban put on his sandals, washed his face and hands, and left the house, running. But after a moment he was back.

"Why do you stand there, woman?" he said to his mother. "Clear the house. Make room for the camels. Spread straw for them, and prepare the best we have for this—stranger."

He left them to their work, which they did as quickly as possible. Rebecca had never seen her stout mother move so fast, and as for herself, her nimble feet and fingers seemed possessed of their own life as they flew about their jobs. Half an hour passed. The outbuildings were cleared, the straw laid. The main area of the household, where guests were received, had been hastily swept, and rugs and skins shaken and spread around the walls. In the cooking room, a fire was kindled and bread and cakes mixed. Rebecca had to go to a neighbor for extra honey and nuts.

And all the time she was sweeping, and carrying, and kneading, and baking, Rebecca's thoughts and feelings were in a tumult. She only felt certain that something irrevocable and tremendous was about to happen to her; but she didn't in the least feel sure that she was ready or that she wanted it.

Before they were fully prepared, they heard voices coming near the house, and the jingling of camel bells. Laban's deep, loud voice dominated the conversation.

"Come in, come in, my honored guest! I have cleared the house and made room for the camels. My mother and sister shall serve you and your men with their own hands."

Rebecca glanced shyly at her mother.

"Not you," her mother whispered swiftly. "Out of sight, finish preparing the cakes, and then go and wash yourself and put on fresh clothes. When you are to show yourself your brother will call you."

"Am I to wear these still?" She held out her arms.

"Would you insult the giver? Wear them, of course. Did you not hear your brother? The man is no stranger, but the messenger of our kinsman Abraham of whom we have often talked. His wealth is beyond counting, as I hear —Go now, quickly. They are coming in."

She pushed Rebecca out of the back door and turned to bring water to wash the stranger's feet, the fat rolls of her face crinkling into a smile of the warmest welcome. . . .

Rebecca did as she'd been told and was back, standing outside the door, in time to hear Eliezer relate his story to Laban. The camels had been unsaddled and were standing knee-deep in the fresh straw near Rebecca, their flexible jaws slowly grinding at the fodder. One of them tried to eat Rebecca's black hair, but she pushed its bony head aside impatiently, afraid to miss a word from within the room.

"And so," concluded Eliezer's voice, "I bowed myself down and gave thanks to my master's God who had led me in the right way to take my master's brother's grandchild for his son."

"It was well you did so," said her brother, in a tone of

propitiating eagerness, almost of fawning, such as she had only heard him use to the richest merchants and such others as could do him good. She cringed inside herself at his manner of speaking. Surely ordinary courtesy, normal good manners were sufficient, even when receiving the greatest? Rebecca did not want this man, this messenger, who held her fate in his hands, to know or guess what she knew of her brother.

The calm voice of Eliezer went on. "And now if you will deal kindly and truly with my master, tell me that I may take your sister back with me. Or if not, tell me *that* also, so that I may know where I stand."

Laban's words seemed to fall from him all confused with anxious windy breath. "The whole matter, you say, is in the hands of your master's God. What then have I to say to it? It is not for a mere brother to interfere in what a god has already ordained." Rebecca could tell that he was prostrating himself on the floor at the stranger's feet, for his voice became muffled. She curled her lip, for she knew her brother had no belief in any gods but his own, whose little statues stood in niches around the walls.

"Let us then ask the maiden," said Eliezer. "In her mouth will be God's fair answer. Let her consent or refusal be the final, proving sign."

Rebecca stiffened, both hands to her face, which felt as if on fire. Only now it came home to her. She was the Lord's elect, chosen to be the wife of Isaac her cousin. Dimly she realized now why she had behaved as she had beside the well. But what did it entail? Not merely marriage. She had often thought of that, longed for it even. It meant leaving her mother, her home, and her friends. . . . And for what? To what? To *whom?* She did not even know how old Isaac might be. If he were the son of her great-uncle, who, as she had always understood, was incredibly old—well over a hundred—surely Isaac must also be a very old man?

But now Laban was clapping his hands as a signal to her to come in. She entered quietly and decorously, keeping her veiled face lowered, and stood silent and awed before Eliezer, who was seated comfortably on the floor eating cakes.

"Come, little maid," he said kindly, peering upward to glimpse her face. "We are old friends by now. We have exchanged gifts—you gave me water, more precious and hard-won than the cold metal I offered you in return, so I am in your debt. Don't be afraid of me."

It is not you, but your master and his son that I fear, thought Rebecca, but of course she said nothing. A quick glance showed that her brother was bowing and grinning and rubbing his hands in a most foolish and unseemly way. Soon she saw why. Eliezer's servants, at a sign from him, were bringing forward the saddle packs and opening them, drawing forth an assortment of the most beautiful objects Rebecca had ever seen. Ornaments of gold and silver, set with bright shining stones, were laid tenderly on a rich cloth spread on the floor, followed by clothes of amazing splendor which drew gasps from the women of the household. Suddenly the awed spell broke, and Rebecca, quite forgetting herself, dropped to her knees to touch and stroke the bright lovely things. Their value she didn't even guess at; they attracted her by their brilliance and beauty, their smoothness to the touch, the magic of the workmanship. . . . Eliezer, seeing her delight, clapped his hands and laughed.

"Come, let me adorn you!" he cried, and picking up a length of cloth the color of ripe apricots, he draped it around her face; then he took up a chain of silver, strung with bell-shaped silver medallions, and hung it on her brow in a crescent.

"See how her eyes shine!" he exclaimed. "The Lord chooses well! My master's grandchildren will be handsome, and he will give me thanks for finding such a bride for his son!"

Rebecca looked at her brother's face for approval, but surprised there a look of such naked greed and avidity that she was filled with shame and quickly took the things off. Eliezer, mistaking the reason, calmed his excitement and said more soberly, "But we go too fast. Precious gifts are but the salt upon the meat of the bargain. I'm sure it is not the custom of this place to marry a maiden to any man, even the very servant of the Lord, against her inclination. Let Rebecca say her will. Come, Rebecca, speak! Will you leave your kindred and come with me across the desert to be the wife of him whose father sent me? Don't let these pretty trinkets sway you. Speak from your woman's heart."

There was a silence in the room, broken only by the sharp, eager breathing of Laban, the strength of whose wish for her to say yes she could actually feel, as if his very hand urged her roughly on. *Oh my brother*, she thought, *you would gladly give your own soul away for only a portion of what lies on that silken cloth! Little you care that my "yes" will rob you of your sister forever.* She looked toward her mother, standing half hidden in the doorway, nodding frantically at her behind Eliezer's back. Rebecca stifled a sigh. For a moment she had a strong desire to thwart them both, well knowing the baseness of their motives. But then she thought, *Not their wishes, nor my own—for how can I wish myself married to a man I have never seen? But God's wish will guide me.*

"I will go," she said.

Once the presents had changed hands, Rebecca's mother and brother began begging Eliezer to let Rebecca stay with them for a few months longer. It was so hard to part with her, they said, and this was true, chiefly because she was the only daughter of the house and did the work of three or four, work which would now fall upon her mother and brother if she went. But Eliezer, who was no fool, had summed up the bride's relatives and concluded it was, in this case as so often, extremely fortunate that the couple would be living at a distance from them. Moreover he was now in a hurry to get back to Abraham with his prize. So he put on his dignity once more and soon Laban was groveling at his feet, urging him to do whatever his wisdom thought best, and the mother was waddling about packing up Rebecca's things and choosing which of their few serving girls should go with her. Seeing them thus, Rebecca found it difficult to dredge up too much sorrow in her heart at the parting.

Just before she left, Laban took her aside.

"Take your brother's blessing," he said, piously putting his hands on her head. She bowed it submissively, though her thoughts were scornful. "May you be happy and prosperous," he went on. "I hope you will bear many sons to this cousin of ours, so that your line will do honor to us all, and strike terror into the hearts of our enemies."

"What enemies?" she asked.

"Every man has his enemies," said Laban grimly. "Go. Be obedient. Be fruitful. Don't forget your family in the good times to come." *Only in the bad*, added Rebecca silently; but then she scolded herself for even secret disrespect. However, when she looked for the last time into the small, crafty eyes of her brother, her emotions were mainly of relief that, at all events, she was free of *his* domination and out of sight of his shaming, dishonest ways.

Isaac was sitting by Be'er-Lehai-Ro-i. Evening was coming. The first faint, cooling breezes of the approaching night were just beginning to drift across the half-shriveled pasture at whose scanty growth the flocks were tearing. The animals, feeling these merciful breezes even through their coarse coats, raised their heads and turned their narrow faces toward it.

Isaac stood up, making throbbing, chirruping noises to the herd. It was past time to start for home. His heart was quiet, his mood mildly elated after the peaceful, uninterrupted day of silence and meditation. He dipped a pot into the well and prepared to drink his fill before starting.

Suddenly the goats turned their heads in the opposite direction, looking north. Isaac turned too. His shadow, and that of the well, and those of the massed animals, stretched out like long dark pools in the sand. Beyond them, quite far away, was a brown cloud moving toward them. Isaac stared. It looked like a camel train. Was that possible? They were not on a regular caravan route. Perhaps they were lost, or perhaps they were coming to visit his father. He hastily dashed the water over his face, wiped it on his neckcloth, and, leaving the herd, began to walk toward the dust cloud with its nucleus of long-legged moving shapes.

Rebecca saw him coming long before he saw her. His tiny black figure grew momentarily taller, broader, more solid. She had a strange feeling that before they met, that figure would grow to gigantic size, would tower over her and encompass her. . . . She rubbed her dust-filled eyes and looked again.

"What man is this coming to meet us?" she asked breathlessly.

Eliezer's old eyes only now spotted the approaching figure. "Why, it's my master's son, your bridegroom!" he exclaimed happily. "That is a good omen, that we meet him here by chance."

Rebecca felt she should be surprised, yet she was not. Somehow she had guessed. . . . She stared and stared. He was not yet close enough for her to see his features, but he was not an old man, that was obvious—he walked so upright, with such vigor in his steps. And his body was tall and well made. And were those not curls on his head, and a fine black beard? She was so busy watching him that it was not until he was within a hundred paces of them that she considered how she must look to him. Never having ridden a camel before, she had been forced to ride astride in the most immodest fashion, with her skirts tucked up. . . . "Stop, stop!" she begged her mount, who plodded on unheeding. "Oh, my lord, do stop it so that I may order my garments and put on my veil!" she cried to Eliezer. Chuckling, he caught her camel's bridle and dragged it to a halt. "Make it lie down!" Rebecca whispered in agony, longing to dismount but terrified of the long drop to the ground. As soon as the beast had bent its legs sufficiently, she tumbled off into the sand, snatched up her veil, and straightened her garments. But how dusty, how filthy she was! She did not at all agree that it was a good omen that her bridegroom should come upon her for the first time in such a state. Oh, if only he *were* old and ugly, it would not matter so much. . . .

She still had her back turned and was despairingly tugging at and brushing her crumpled, sand-dusted skirt when she heard a deep male voice say, "Well, Eliezer! Where have you been, and who is this girl that you bring with you? Have you been on an illicit expedition with my father's best camels to fetch a new wife for your old age?"

Rebecca caught the note of jesting in his voice and clasped her hands to her throat with a gasp almost of rapture. "Oh, if we could but make each other laugh!" she thought. Laughter had been a rarity indeed in her home, for Laban was a stranger to levity and jokes, having his mind always bent upon gain, and considering Rebecca's flashes of fun impious and disrespectful.

She whirled around, unable any longer to control her desire to see Isaac. Flattened against the camel's side, she gazed at him over her veil. But he was—beautiful! A most beautiful man. Not young, about forty she guessed, but strong, fine-featured, with kind eyes and a strange, gentle mouth such as she had never seen on a man before—a mouth that could never issue shouts or sharp words. A face to love and trust oneself to. She knew in that first glance that she was going to love him with the whole of herself, and she offered thanks on the spot to God for the blessing of such a husband, who could arouse in her this feeling of devotion. It never crossed her mind that the blessing of that kind of love could turn into a curse.

Isaac's reaction to Rebecca and to the sudden news, for which he had not been prepared, that he was to marry her, was by no means so wholehearted and simple as her reaction to him.

To begin with, he had very profound reasons for not wanting to marry. He was deeply afraid of love, and had always, since his mother's death, kept himself out of reach of it. Of course on the other hand he knew that he must marry sometime, and beget children—that was inevitable since his father had no other heir; but he had hoped to postpone it as long as possible, and, when he had forced himself to contemplate it, had comforted himself with the thought that many marriages were merely unions of convenience. Love was not necessary; children could be procreated without it. A sense of duty and a healthy body, together with God's blessing, were sufficient for that. To this end—the end of keeping his heart free—he had hinted to his father several times that he would prefer a plain, or even uncomely, woman.

And now—this. He saw her eyes, her figure. . . . He would not look further.

He led her to his father, who unveiled her, and a slow, tender smile spread over the old man's face.

"My son," he said, "you have often told me that you were not ambitious for a beautiful wife. Now you see how those who are most humble in their demands are rewarded

by God. For since I beheld the face of my beloved Sarah in
her youth, I have not seen such a fair young creature. God
has indeed been good to you to rear up such a flower to
grace the tent of his favorite."

Putting his gnarled hands on Rebecca's shoulders, he
turned her around to face his son. Isaac dared one look,
then covered his eyes in despair.

"Oh, God!" he prayed in silent anguish. "What
would you do to me? When I look at her, I forget all, even
the cold edge of the knife on my throat. I forget even my
own dearest mother. Where is my sorrow, where is my
prudence, where is my caution? God, if you love me, hear
me now before I look again upon her! I will be good to
her, and beget children upon her, and guard her honor and
theirs with all the strength that is in me. But spare me from
loving her, spare me from loving my sons that will come
out of her! Do this, reserve my heart, and I will turn it to
worship you. My heart and mind shall be yours, even as
my father's were. Let me only not suffer as he suffered
when he led me into the mountain!"

He waited a moment for the tumult in his heart to die
down, and then slowly he lowered his hands. The face before him was drenched with tears, but not one particle less
enchanting for that. Rather, those tears, which he knew he
had caused by refusing to look at her, made him want to
run and embrace her, to kiss her lips, to assure her that she
was all any man could desire, that he had hidden her from
his sight because she was *too* beautiful. . . .

"What are you waiting for, my son? She is yours.
Take her. House her in your mother's tent, that has stood
empty all these years. It has been prepared for you. . . .
God be praised! I am the happiest man . . . the happiest
man. . . ."

And old Abraham sank back among his cushions with
a look of inexpressible joy and peace on his face.

So Isaac led Rebecca to his mother's tent. A feast had

been prepared for them within—their first meal together. Her hands trembling with delight, she served him. He sat on the ground cross-legged, his eyes cast down, eating as stolidly as if she were some coarse-limbed serving maid. Undismayed, thinking that this no doubt was the correct way for a new-wed husband to behave, Rebecca seated herself near his feet.

"May I eat?" she asked when his meal was finished.

The sound of her voice sent thrills of anguish through him. He longed to arrange the cushions for her, to put morsels of food in her mouth with his own fingers, to stroke her black hair and feast his eyes on her face. Words of love sprang into his mouth. He throttled them back.

"Do as you will," he said.

She ate silently. The indifference in his tone had chilled her. She kept glancing at him. Why did he keep his eyes fixed on his feet and his hands locked together? Was he perhaps afraid of *her* in some way? She understood that a man, even a man past the shyness of boyhood, might be nervous on such an occasion. It was surely for her, then, to sooth his qualms, to give him such proofs of her love and willingness that his uncertainties would be overcome.

Quite without experience in the ways of grown-up love, Rebecca let her feminine instincts show her the way. Approaching him with all due modesty, she began to talk to him, gently and timidly letting her fingers touch him here and there. He did not pull away or rebuke her, so she grew bolder.

She began to speak about her life with her family in Aram; she made little jokes about her brother's greedy ways, and then she told him about her meeting with Eliezer. She even ventured to tell him how she had tried to work out his age from his father's, and hinted at her relief and delight at seeing, as he walked toward her through the field, that he was not old, but young and handsome. . . .

"I am old enough to be your father," he said flatly.

Rebecca laughed aloud. "I can't think of you and my father in the same thought. He was gray and stooped and always irritable. . . . Tell me you will not be often angry with me, as he was; for if you will, I may as well get back on the camel and ride home." To make sure he knew she was teasing, she dared, very softly, to tug his hair.

He threw her a quick look which she did not understand at all—it seemed to be a look of pain, yet she knew she had not hurt him. Very gently she said, "Is anything the matter, my husband? If something troubles your heart, whether it concerns me or not, you should tell it to me." And this time she put her hand into his, for calling him "my husband" seemed to confirm that she was indeed his wife and might be bold in seeking to comfort him.

Isaac stood up suddenly and moved away from her. After a few moments' silence, he said in a muffled voice, "This was my mother's tent."

"Was it?"

"It has not been used since—she died."

"And is that long ago?"

"More than twenty years."

This was longer than she had lived. She glanced around her at the walls of the tent and saw that they were ancient and cracked, despite their finery. She felt a sense of awe and uneasiness.

"Did she die—in here?"

"Yes."

Ah! Now she thought she understood. Perhaps her husband thought that his mother's spirit hovered near them and might be displeased by their nuptials. She rose up and stood beside him.

"Do you think your mother might not approve of me?"

Now he looked at her fully; when he opened his fine eyes upon her, the pain in them was unmistakable, and she shrank back a step.

"You do! You do!" she cried softly.

"No. How could she not approve? You are—" he stopped.

"Then what? What is it? What is wrong?"

He heard the tears in her voice and felt compassion and love twist in him like a spear.

"I—I still grieve for her," he muttered, trying to take his eyes off her, trying to subdue his feelings, trying with all his strength to remember the last time he had been in this tent. . . . But it had faded. His grief was no longer solid.

Rebecca had lowered her hands from her face and was gazing at him in childish surprise.

"After so many years you can still grieve?" she asked.

"It has always weighed on me. It always will," he said, desperately wanting it to be true.

"No, no, my husband! Of course it won't! Did she not love you? Could it be her wish that you should sorrow for her forever and shun all comfort? I know what must be the wish of her spirit, if it still haunts this tent. It has waited all this time to see you consoled, to see her son made happy again. Come! It is time to give up your sadness, to let it float away. It's not God's will that any man should mar his whole life, and his joy in marriage, for a natural sorrow twenty years old. Let it go! Come. Come to me."

She held out her arms. Isaac felt himself lost, as if her flowery breath and the touch of her mouth were the lapping of encroaching quicksands, rising to engulf him forever. He struggled to free himself, not from the circle of her arms—indeed that was so light and tender a clasp that he could have thrown it off in a moment—but from the passionate sensations that were threatening to drown him. It was useless . . . his body acted without his will, gathering the lithe soft female creature against him and performing with her all the rites of wedlock. Again and again, while he did so, he repeated despairingly to himself the words, "To get children! Only to get children!" But it was not only for that, and he knew, now, that he had been an ignorant fool to suppose himself capable of performing this act primarily for any purpose but his own present pleasure. What confounded him was his conviction, which no amount of mental struggle then or later could overcome, that this pleasure with Rebecca was not base and animal, but holier than prayer.

Isaac took Rebecca to Be'er-Lehai-Ro-i, and there raised a beautiful tent for her, roomy enough to shelter the large family which they both confidently expected to have. For a year, two years, they were happy, in a strange way. But that happiness was based, not on their love for each other, but on their expectation that this love would be fruitful. Only in this hope could Isaac justify the way he felt and acted toward Rebecca, for when he was not actually making love to her he could still convince himself that his love was physical and that spiritually he was free and unencumbered, that he was still safe—he could not believe that God had not answered his prayer to protect him from the more dangerous, spiritual love of which he was so afraid.

As for Rebecca, she adored Isaac passionately, so much so that for months she ignored in him all signs that he was withholding his love from her. She put his coldness of manner down to a lingering sorrow for his mother. Because, when they were alone together at night, he turned to her in such a frenzy of need and desire, she felt sure that little by little he would come to show his love for her all the time. In any case, she was certain that their children, when they came, would serve to bind them together.

But God, it seemed, had forgotten them.

Isaac grew morose, and nurtured deep, unsharable fears. Was this denial his own fault? In praying that he

might be spared the pangs of loving his children, had he in
fact been praying not to have any?

Happiness and hope do not change to misery and despair overnight. It took years to reduce them to a condition
of utter wretchedness, quite comparable to that of Abraham and Sarah during her decades of barrenness. The
laughter and gaiety went out of Rebecca. She felt ashamed,
cheated, disgraced. Her arms ached for a child to hold; her
heart simmered in bafflement and loneliness.

At last she began to keep herself from Isaac, and he
knew the time had come to be open with her.

"Rebecca," he said to her one night when they lay
side by side, wrapped in their separate thoughts, "let us
share our hearts."

She turned her head toward him.

"Can *you* say that? My heart has been yours to share
from the beginning."

"It is not so lately."

"No."

"Rebecca, my heart is not like yours. We are like a
day and a night in the desert—hot and cold. You have
warmed me, but I have chilled you. I am sorry, but it's
what I am. I cannot help it."

"This desert cold has not only chilled my heart, but
my blood too," said Rebecca, turning her back on him.

"No, wife, don't turn from me! Listen, for now I
want to confess to you. Would it not warm us both if we
could have a child?"

After a long silence, Rebecca said, "Of what use is it to
say that? You only wound me with the word 'child.' I am
barren."

"What if—what if I told you that I thought you could
not be truly barren? God chose you as my bride, and God
promised that my father should people this land with his
seed, through me. What, then? If you secretly fear that I
will despair of you and take other wives, put it from you,

for I will not—I am not such a fool as to follow my father along *that* track, for I know where it leads."

Rebecca, listening incredulously, half turned back toward him, for his words were wine and balm to her soul. "So why, you ask, has God forgotten us? I think he is punishing me," Isaac went on.

"For what sin?"

"It was a sin of thought—a sin of cowardice, I see that now. And how should I see it, if not that God has opened my eyes? So now we will get up, and kneel together, and I will pray that this curse may be lifted from us—from me. I will beg pardon of God for my blasphemy."

"Tell me what you did. I must know."

"I prayed—" he began. He stopped, then went on. "I prayed that I might be spared loving my children. For my father loved me, and my mother also, far more than is usual, and see how God put their love to the test! Better, far better not to love . . . And yet . . ."

"Oh, you fool! You fool!" cried Rebecca. "For this God may never forgive you! For this *I* am punished! For this *I* am accursed!" She rocked and moaned. Suddenly she stopped. "Did you wish—also—to be spared loving me?"

"No! No!" Isaac lied, for he was afraid to tell her the truth.

Rebecca stared at him. "If you did," she said slowly, "you do not deserve me. And I have thrown my love down a well." He forced himself to meet her searching eyes, and at last, though only half convinced, she sighed. "Come. Let us talk no more, but do as you said. And let me hear you pray with all your might. Swear to open your heart, no matter what pain creeps in." A sort of feverish exasperation came over her, and she scolded. "Say you will welcome the pain. Who has ever heard of children without pain! Oh, I cannot believe that even a man can be so blind and stupid. What would you think of my wits and my goodness if I prayed to have children, yet be spared the pangs of bearing them? Children *are* pain. All joy must be paid for in pain. You might as well question God's design by praying for endless day." Isaac, kneeling before her, hung his head. "Pray, my husband! Intercede for me in my barrenness, before I forget myself and intercede for *you* in your folly!"

He felt her strength, her sureness flowing into him. He bowed himself to the ground and humbled himself before God, "with all his might" as she had said. And that very night, Rebecca conceived.

It was no easy, happy pregnancy such as Sarah's. The laughter that had been Sarah's at that time, and Rebecca's since babyhood, died out of her, driven away by the endless pain and sickness.

So ill did she become toward the end that she went to consult the midwife.

"Do all women suffer so?" she asked.

The midwife examined her. Her face was tinged with gray, her eyes embedded in dark pits, her body emaciated, emphasizing the vastness of her belly. Kneeling before her, the old woman pressed her ear to this protuberance, listened carefully on one side, then on the other. Then she felt it with her fingers.

"You carry two within you," she said at last.

"I had guessed," and Rebecca wearily. "Sometimes I have thought they must be at war with each other, for they seem to thresh and struggle in my womb. If it is thus before they are born, what peace will we know when they are grown?" Her whole body seemed to be jolted from within, and she clasped both hands over her belly. "Softly, my little ones, be friends!" she whispered. "Oh, how I dread the birth, yet how I wish it would come! I fear neither will give place to the other, and that they will emerge side by side."

The midwife could not help chuckling at such an idea. "Nay, nay, it cannot be. Be easy. I shall be with you. If they try any tricks upon me, I shall hold the smaller back to make way for the bigger. For the firstborn must be the stronger as he will be my lord's heir."

That night Rebecca had a dream in which, for the first time, God spoke to her. It seemed to her that He came and laid His hands one on each side of her belly and said, "Two nations are in thy womb. And two peoples shall be born of thee. And the one people shall be stronger than the other people. And the elder shall serve the younger."

She gave a great deal of thought to this strange dream, and asked Isaac about it. Isaac said it must have been the midwife's words that had given her this dream, for God's decree from the most ancient times had always been that the firstborn should inherit.

A short time after this, the twins were born.

The birth was not hard. Rebecca was fully aware, and able, as the first child was born, to half sit up and see him emerge. He was the strangest baby she had ever seen; even the midwife started at the sight of him, for he was not only red all over but covered with a fine growth of hair like a young animal.

As he was born into the midwife's hands, one foot did not come free. It seemed to be caught. The old woman tugged it briskly, but Rebecca cried in her pain, "Don't! The other is coming!"

"So soon?" murmured the old woman. "One should not follow thus, without respite for the mother, so sharp upon the other's heel." And her words were truer than she knew, for a few moments later the second child was born. And this was stranger still; for instead of coming out headfirst, the first part to emerge was his hand, and it was closed tightly upon the heel of the other. The midwife had to gather them up together; she wiped them with oil and laid them, head-to-foot, in the place prepared for them.

But until they had ceased squalling and fallen asleep, she was not able to disengage the tiny grip and separate them.

Isaac was not so much delighted as overwhelmed by this double answer to his prayers. Twin boys, both strong and healthy! He hung over them, gazing at their sleeping figures in wonder. The face of the eldest stirred him strangely.

"This hairiness—"

"It will pass," said the midwife.

"It gives him the look of a grown man. And why is he so red?"

She shrugged. "The birth struggle, perhaps."

The smaller face caused him no qualms. No angry redness here, or precocious look. A baby's face, wrinkled and touching in sleep . . . Isaac stroked the clenched fist, no bigger than a walnut, and the minute fingers opened and clutched one of his.

"What a grip!" he exclaimed with all a father's pride.

"His brother's heel bears witness to that," said the midwife, and, uncovering the other's foot, showed the imprints of five little bruises. "Indeed, he did not mean to be the last-born, and would have held his elder back if he could, and preceded him."

"Then let us call this one Jacob," said Isaac, forming a name from the Hebrew word for "heel." "And the elder shall be called Esau"—which means, fully-formed, because he already had the look of a man.

Esau never shed his hair, as most babies do. He kept it, and as he grew, so the hair on his body and head grew thicker and stronger. And his father, who had at first been dismayed by this, now saw in it a source of great pride.

"My heir was a man from the beginning," he would say.

Esau was, from the first, the stronger and more masculine of the two. Even as a young boy, hunting was his chief delight. He also loved to wrestle, and would lurk and pounce upon Jacob, rolling him on the ground and forcing him to submit to his will. At the age of ten he slew his first gazelle, and bore it back in triumph to his father.

Isaac's eyes glistened. "Well done, my son! You will be a great hunter! And for your first kill, you have hit upon the creature that gives my favorite meat."

Jacob, anxious to have a share in his father's praise, offered to cook it, and Rebecca let him try, at least to the extent of leaving him alone to watch it as it roasted. But Jacob was a dreamer; the fire burned low while he thought himself into Esau's hairy skin and imagined himself the best-loved of his father, and when he was brought back to himself by a sharp word from his mother, the meat was already spoiled and tough.

Esau was enraged. His first kill, made specially to delight his father by providing a delicious meal—ruined. He waited till his mother's back was turned and then, seizing Jacob, gave him a severe beating.

Rebecca and Isaac heard the uproar and came rushing to separate them. Rebecca wrested Jacob from the punishing grasp of his much stronger brother, while Isaac pinioned Esau's arms.

"He did it on purpose!" panted Esau, struggling to free himself.

"I didn't, I didn't," Jacob sobbed, while his mother wiped the blood from his mouth with a corner of her robe.

Isaac tried to sooth Esau. "I understand why you were so angry—to have your treat for me spoiled. But—"

Rebecca rounded on them both, holding Jacob protectively in her arms. "You understand! What degree of cruelty would you *not* understand, if it were Esau's doing? You favor him unjustly! You favor him so that if you saw him killing my boy, you would excuse him somehow! This one is no ruffian, no savage fighter. He is gentle, gentle as the harmless deer that this mighty hunter, here, takes such pride in slaughtering. I will not stand by and see my Jacob suffer at the hands of this my other son who, to his mother's sorrow at least, is a bully!"

Esau had stopped struggling and was staring in astonishment at his mother. Isaac stared too. It was the first time Rebecca had so openly declared her preference. Later, when the twins were asleep, he taxed her with it.

"It is not good to make it so clear that you prefer the younger to the elder," he said.

"And what of you?" she responded instantly. "Is it better to favor Esau, and to let Jacob feel continually that he counts for nothing with you?"

"That is untrue! I see the virtues and failings of each." Rebecca gave him a scornful look. "If Esau is nearer to my heart, is that not his proper place as my heir?" Isaac added, aware that he was contradicting himself but struggling to be truthful.

"That aside, you prefer him. Why, I don't know, for Jacob is far more like you, except that he is more affectionate, more warmhearted—"

"He shows but few signs of approaching manhood. He would rather stay in the tent and help you with the cooking than go out hunting. It's true he's good with the sheep, but that is the least one expects. And if Esau is a fighter, what of that? A boy should enjoy his strength and cunning."

"You choose your words well, my lord. Esau *is* cunning, cunning and sly."

"That at least I can deny. Jacob is the sly one. He uses his wits to make up for his deficiencies in strength and courage."

"We shall see," said Rebecca, controlling her anger with an effort. "We shall see which of them will triumph when they are men—Esau with his brute strength and ill nature, or Jacob, who is all heart and brain."

Isaac looked at her with puzzled, half-suspicious eyes.

"What do you mean, 'triumph?' Esau was born the elder. Nothing, no flaw in him or virtue in Jacob, can alter that."

"We shall see," said Rebecca again enigmatically.

The truth of the matter was that Jacob, with his open-hearted, boyish love for her, had won from his mother's half-starved heart all the burden of affection that she had not been able to spill upon Isaac. In Jacob she saw her husband all over again, the same dark beauty, the same gentleness, the same reserved, thoughtful nature; but combined with it was an ability to love fully and completely which had never been Isaac's.

They doted on each other, and Esau, who, despite his brutishness, was not unfeeling and would have liked to be his mother's as well as his father's favorite, saw and was envious. As he grew up, he cultivated his father's preference. Isaac was aging now; it seemed unlikely that he would live to be as old as his father Abraham, who had only recently died at a very great age. Isaac's eyes were already growing dim and his limbs weak. He let his sons manage his herds, and Esau did most of the hunting for the family. Isaac liked food, and as he lost the other pleasures of life his interest in eating became a passion with him. Esau was careful to minister to this.

One day Jacob and Esau quarreled about this matter of serving food to their father.

"I take all the risks," said Esau. "What good would all your womanish talents be if I did not bring you the game? I know full well you gain my father's praise undeservedly for dressing the meat, when really our mother does most of it and lets you pretend it was you. You're forever trying to steal Father's love for me."

Jacob quite liked to see Esau working himself up into a rage of this sort. It never came to blows between them now that they were grown up; Esau scorned to lay hands on his brother, whom he regarded as little better than a woman in his weakness and lack of spirit. So Jacob just smiled at Esau's railing and went on measuring lentils for the soup he was going to make.

"What nonsense is that you are about now?" shouted Esau, made angrier by Jacob's lack of response.

"What is it to you? It will be good and you will be glad enough to eat it."

"I do not eat slops. If there is no meat for our evening meal, say so, and I shall go out with my bow and get game."

"Kill a sheep."

"My father does not delight in mutton as he does in venison. I will hunt a deer. Keep in a good fire, little *sister*, and reserve the pap for those of our household who have lost their teeth."

Jacob glanced up at him with an expression Esau could not read but did not care for. Then he quietly began pouring the lentils into the pot. Esau, frustrated, turned on his heel and went out.

He hunted for hours without success. When he was still far from home, dark clouds climbed the sky over his head and, opening with a flash, poured down rain in torrents. He bit his wet lips in fury. There was no hope of finding a quarry now. With the water sluicing down his almost furry shoulders, he headed for home. Suddenly he stopped. A lone gazelle, caught in the open by the storm, bounded across his path, lit up by flashes of lightning. Esau raised his bow in an instant, hope in his heart; but the strange light baffled his aim. His shaft went wide and the creature vanished in a series of wild leaps.

Esau reached home in a black rage. He had not broken his fast all day, and hunger, combined with disappointment, quite unmanned him. When he lifted the tent flap and smelled the lentil stew simmering with herbs and chunks of lamb, he felt himself slavering at the mouth. The sight of Jacob, calm, dry, warm, self-satisfied, stirring the savory-smelling pot, nearly drove Esau wild, for he came empty-handed and must now depend on his brother for the meal he had to have.

"Give me food, brother, for I faint with hunger," he said shortly.

Jacob looked up at him with those unreadable, calm dark eyes. "Oh. So I am your brother now. You called me otherwise before."

"Has our mother not taught us that every word need not be taken seriously?" Esau asked.

"Were you joking then?"

"Of course! Come. Feed me. I famish."

"Give me the game you went to hunt and I will prepare it for you to bite upon with your strong teeth. I'm sure you will not like this—slop," said Jacob, who, in one look, had summed up the results of Esau's excursion.

"I care not what it is, give it to me now before I am forced to take it," said Esau between clenched teeth.

Jacob calmly continued stirring and, after a silence which quite maddened Esau, said slowly, "Our father will be displeased if we fight and the soup gets spilled. Besides, there's no need. There is plenty here for us all. Bring a dish and I will give you all you want."

Esau flung himself across the tent to the pile of earthenware bowls and, choosing the biggest, brought it to the fireside, where he stood with it in his hands like a beggar, feeling anger and humiliation burning in his breast.

"Food?" he shouted, thrusting the bowl forward.

"Softly, brother," said Jacob. "All in good time. First there is a small matter I want to discuss with you."

"What matter? I tell you I am starving!"

"Careful, do not jostle me! I may spill the soup. The matter is that of your birthright."

"Birthright?"

"Yes, yes! Your inheritance as the eldest son."

Esau gazed at him, his hunger for a moment forgotten. "What of it?"

"Do you care for it?"

"Care for it? What does that mean? It's mine, I don't have to care for it. Why are you making me wait?" And he pushed the bowl forward again.

"It seems likely to me that you don't give it much thought," said Jacob slowly. "Yet I think often that I would like the birthright to be mine. It matters little to you, but it would mean a lot to me. Therefore I suggest that you sell it to me."

Esau's brain did not work very quickly, especially when he was so hungry. He stood with his mouth open. At last he licked his lips.

"Sell? For what?"

Jacob lifted the ladle in the pottage and let the savory stuff pour back into the pot. Esau swallowed as he looked at it.

"For this," he said.

"But—but—" struggled Esau, "that is only food."

"*Only* food, brother? Is food then so little to you? Shall I tip the pot and let it pour out upon the coals?"

"No!"

"Without food, we lose our strength. Do you not feel your strength ebbing away? Do you not see that I am the strong one now, because the food is with me? Listen, Esau. What do you want with the birthright? What does it mean? All the rights of the eldest are not pleasures. Many are duties, duties to our father and to God far more onerous than going out hunting occasionally. You pretend to be pious, but in fact you care little for God. All the rites and sacrifices you will owe to Him when our father dies will be nothing but a nuisance to you, whereas I will do them gladly. Sell me your birthright, and go your ways, not merely filled in body but free in soul. Come." Jacob reached up and took Esau's bowl. "See how I fill it to the brim. Here is bread to eat it with. Now say the birthright is mine, and in another moment it will fill your mouth and comfort all your nature. For your nature is of the earth and the flesh, and mine is of the spirit. It was only by chance, or perhaps by superior strength even then, that you came first from our mother's womb. We can now rectify the matter sensibly between ourselves. Speak! Do you agree?"

"Yes—I agree! Anything. Only give me the food!"

But for a moment longer, Jacob held it across the fire, beyond the reach of Esau's outstretched hands.

"Swear," he said, in such a solemn tone that Esau was checked.

But then Esau thought, "What force has this agreement? Our father will never ratify it, and if he gives the elder's blessing to me, as he assuredly will, near his life's end, this compact will mean nothing at all." So he swore, and grabbed the food, gulping it down in an ecstasy while Jacob sat quietly watching him.

Satisfied at last, Esau laid down the bowl and smiled at Jacob. He felt now warm and full and benign.

"So, brother, how does it feel to be the elder? Is it as good as being filled with good victuals?"

"Almost as good," replied Jacob, smiling. But Esau was too sleepy to hear the note of irony, and fell asleep quite confident that he had got the best of the bargain.

Years passed. The family traveled about, seeking new pastures, and had a number of strange adventures. There were quarrels with neighboring tribes about water rights, and when these quarrels came to blows, Esau was like a spear and shield to his family. Yet during times of peace, his

fierce, coarse nature was a trial to them all; even Isaac had
cause to rebuke him, though not for picking quarrels with
Jacob, for the two brothers were now as unlike twins as
could well be, not only in looks and characters but in
affections. They avoided each other, and went their separate ways. Esau was like some great dog who could easily
savage his master to death but is held in check through
some subtle fear of another kind of superiority. If enmity
did show itself between them, Jacob had only to look at
Esau in a certain way and make some remark about food
and Esau was quelled. It was something odd that neither of
their parents could ever understand.

Esau was the first to marry. He took two wives, both
of the Hittite tribe. Rebecca opposed this with all her
strength and urged Isaac to oppose it too.

"It is a disaster!" she exclaimed. "No less. With all the
trouble your father took to find you a wife from among his
own people, you allow our blood to be contaminated with
that of these idol worshipers. These men whose daughters
our son now wants to marry were till recently your sworn
enemies! How can you sit there so complacently and allow
it?"

But Isaac could not rouse himself to object. "God has
renewed to me His promise that our seed shall inherit all
this country where we live," he said. "He has said nothing
to me about choosing a wife for Esau. He is well grown.
He can choose for himself. If it is against God's will, let
Him prevent it."

So Esau brought home his two wives, and Rebecca did
her best not to loathe them both, but it was useless. They
were coarse, primitive girls, without culture or grace. To
Jacob alone did she complain. "How could he? How could
he so lower himself to choose such base women?" But
Jacob only shrugged and answered, "They suit him,
Mother. Can't you see that? How would he manage with

delicate, pious, cultivated girls? Only yesterday I saw him strike one of them and knock her down, and she got up again at once and went about her work. They are like working beasts to him, and that is what he needs. A girl to your taste, or mine, he would kill in a week of days."

Rebecca caressed him tenderly and said, "Never mind, my son. When you are minded to marry, I myself will make the arrangements."

At last Isaac became really feeble and almost blind. Rebecca nursed him dutifully and kindly, but in fact all her heart's love was now centered on Jacob, and her greatest sorrow, if she had faced herself honestly, was not that Isaac must one day die, but that when he did, Jacob would receive only a younger son's portion. Then she would see Esau lording it over him, and Esau's detestable, uncouth wives would hold sway over *her* domains. Such a notion was almost intolerable to her. It worked in her brain day and night until finally she convinced herself that Esau, by everything he had ever done, had proved himself unfit for the honors that his birth entitled him to. But what to do about it, she did not know.

Jacob, as an unmarried man, still lived in the old quarters, while Esau and his wives inhabited separate tents. Thus Jacob and Rebecca were together more than ever, and grew closer and closer, at last revealing to each other their greatest secrets.

When Rebecca told Jacob her thoughts about himself, Esau, and what would happen after Isaac's approaching death, Jacob kissed her and said, "Don't distress yourself, Mother! I wish you had told me before what was worrying you. It will not be as you think, for years ago Esau sold me his birthright." And he told her the whole story.

Rebecca was quite beside herself with joy. She kissed

Jacob again and again, praising him for his cleverness and berating Esau for his stupidity and blindness to true values. "So what care I who he marries!" she exulted. "No wonder the Lord did not interfere! For now you shall be the heir, and it is through you that the prophecies shall come true—you, my dear, good, clever son!" And then she remembered the dream she had had just before their birth, in which it was predicted that "the elder should serve the younger," and in breathless excitement she related it to Jacob. "So you see, that proves that this outcome was God's intention from the beginning!"

"But all is not plain and clear yet," Jacob said. "God evidently expects that we shall solve one more problem, and that is—how shall my father be brought to ratify me and repudiate Esau? He will never do it of his own will. We must somehow bring it about."

Rebecca sobered quickly at this new problem, and set her ingenious mind to work to solve it. A solution of sorts soon presented itself, but violent qualms of conscience impeded her in her efforts to work it all out thoroughly. Could it be right—could it be anything but most wickedly wrong, in fact—thus to deceive the husband who had always, within his emotional limits, been good and honest to her? Many sleepless nights were passed in wrestling with herself and praying to God for guidance. But if God tried to guide her in a direction opposed to her inclinations, He failed. In the end she reasoned thus:

"God is above us all. He has performed miracles to bring about His design for us. If He wished Esau to triumph, He would not have made him as he is; He would not have let him marry as he has; He would not have allowed him to sell his birthright to Jacob for a mess of pottage. Nor would He have put into my mind such a design as I have now conceived, of how to bring about a final transfer of the rights of the firstborn to my younger son Jacob."

In that way, she forced her conscience to be quiet and let her think.

One day shortly after this, Isaac woke up feeling lighter and less feeble than he had for some years. Supposing that this lightening was the change before death, he called Esau to him early in the morning.

"Esau," he said, "give me your hand."

Esau readily put his powerful, hirsute hand in his father's two aged ones. Isaac stroked it gently.

"I like to feel your hand in mine," he said. "All the strength, all the vigor of manhood that I never really achieved, is here in this great arm. . . . How much of the good salt tastes of life I missed through being afraid. . . . But you are not like that. You are all the man I was not. Esau, I can no longer see you; my life, like my eyes, is growing dim. Be my good son and take your weapons and go and kill for me a deer, that I may taste that rich, strong meat once more before I die. Then I will give you my blessing."

Esau stood up and looked down at his father for a moment. A strong feeling of sadness rose to his throat so that he could almost have wept. He was glad of it, for it proved he loved the old man and was not anxious for him to die. At the same time he was relieved that he was, after all, to get the elder son's blessing. His compact with Jacob had always troubled him, and more so since his marriage, for of course his wives expected him to inherit and would abuse him in all the subtle ways of women if they found he had cheated them.

"I will go, Father," he said.

As he left the tent, he thought he saw his mother's robe, whisking around a corner. "So she has been listening," he thought. "Well, what matter? She cannot prevent my getting the blessing now." And he went off with his bow and a determination to return only with the finest piece of venison in the area, so as to deserve his father's love.

Rebecca, meanwhile, was shaking Jacob awake.

"Get up, get you up at once or all is lost! Go out now into the pasture and choose two young kids, and bring them to me."

"What for, what has happened?"

"Your father thinks he is dying. He has commanded Esau to go and hunt the deer for his last meal, and by this Esau will earn the blessing. But he will not earn it, for you are to have it instead, as is your *right*," she whispered emphatically.

"But what is to be done? What with the kids?"

"I shall prepare them in such a way that your father shall not know them from venison. In a strong sauce they are much alike. And you shall carry the dish to him, and get his blessing instead of Esau. By the time he comes back, it will all be over."

She and Jacob looked at each other, then each turned away his eyes.

"But he will know me," said Jacob uneasily.

"Speak in a muffled voice. His ears begin to betray him as well as his eyes."

"But the sense of touch he still has. Will he not touch me? Then he must know at once, from my smoothness, that I am not Esau."

"I have thought of that. We will put the skin of the kid on your hands, and on your neck. He will feel this and it will seem to him like the hairiness of your brother."

Again their eyes met, but this time Jacob forced her to keep on looking at him.

"Mother, now we have come to the point I am not easy. Can this deception be right?"

"It is right."

"If my father should guess, he would curse me through all my days."

Rebecca stood up, her heart beating fiercely, for her mind was made up and now Jacob's doubts only irritated her, for time was passing. "Listen, Jacob. If there is any wrong, let it be upon me. If there be any curse, I take it upon me. Close your mind to all doubts, for I have endured and conquered them all for you. Listen only to my voice, and go quickly and get the kids."

Jacob obeyed her. He wanted to; he had intended to— his stirrings of conscience were so frail that his mother's strong assurances quickly scotched them. He ran his hands over the kids' backs till he found one whose coat was not too coarse; that and another he hurriedly manhandled to the slaughtering area, and dispatched them. Then, slinging one across each shoulder, he ran with them to the fireside where Rebecca was piling the pieces of dried dung and charcoal up to make a good red cooking heat.

While she cooked, he kept watch, hoping that ill luck would dog his brother's hunt and delay his return. It took a long time to prepare the dish, for Rebecca had to make the gravy with great care, tasting and re-tasting to make sure the flavor and aroma were strong enough to disguise the flesh. At last she ladled the steaming portion into a decorated dish, and set it to cool a little while she cut out patches of the kids' hide and fastened them to Jacob's hands and neck.

"Wait," she said. "You must wear his clothes."

She fetched from Esau's tent his finest garments, such as he would choose on such an occasion. The two bovine wives looked up at her sullenly as she came in, but she ignored them. She dressed Jacob herself, adjusted the patches of hide, and then, putting her hands on his shoulders, looked into his face.

"It is God's will," she said solemnly.

"We must hope so," said Jacob. "If it is not, most surely one of us will suffer for it."

"Not you, my best beloved," she said. She kissed him, then took up the dish and put it in his hands. "Go now, and remember to speak unclearly. Do not tremble. Do not fear."

"I neither tremble nor fear, Mother," said Jacob calmly. "I have always known that my destiny had gone awry and that I must set it straight."

With that he went into his father's tent. Rebecca crept close to the flap to listen.

"My father," said Jacob.

"Here am I," replied Isaac, sounding rather puzzled. "Who is it?"

"Esau."

"Esau?" repeated the old man.

"I've done as you told me. Come over here and sit and eat the venison I've brought you, and then give me your blessing."

"You've been very quick," said his father, and now he sounded definitely suspicious.

"God was with me and gave me a fine young buck before I had fairly started out from the camp."

There was silence, during which Rebecca clutched her throat and did not breathe. Then the old man said slowly, "Come here." Another pause, and then, "The voice is the voice of Jacob, but the hands are the hands of Esau." His old voice trembled with bewilderment. "Who are you? Which are you?" he asked shrilly.

"I am your first-born, Esau," said Jacob, his voice quiet and steady.

"Are you really Esau?"

"Yes."

"Bring me the venison."

There was a long silence. Then Isaac said again querulously, "Are you truly my son Esau? For there is something even in these hairy hands which is not of him. They are hairy, it's true; but they have not his power. Besides, they smell strange, like an animal."

"It is from killing the buck."

"The meat is good, though," said the old man.

Rebecca relaxed a little, though she was still very tense. The whole scheme suddenly seemed to her beyond reason. How *could* Isaac be deceived? Blind and feeble he might be, but he was not yet foolish. If he felt the hands carefully . . . Rebecca offered up a desperate prayer. "Lord, only you can deceive him! Our paltry disguise cannot do it. Let him give Jacob the blessing, for my son Esau is unworthy—" She was interrupted by Isaac's voice.

"Good! Good! Is there wine? Ah!" And then, "Now, come near me, my son, and kiss me . . . Yes, I know this cloth, this headpiece . . . This strange smell is strong about your face, too . . . Esau—are you Esau? Say once more that you are, I want to believe you, for I hate a lie."

And again Jacob said firmly, "I am Esau, Father."

Rebecca heard the old man sigh heavily. Then he said, "Kneel down then, and I'll bless you."

The blessing that came from his lips was so beautiful that Rebecca was struck dumb as she listened.

"My son smells of the field, of the hunt in which God has blessed him. God give His blessings to my son; let them rain down on him like dew. God bless him with the rich things of the earth, the corn, and the wine. My son, may nations serve and bow down to you, for you are lord over all your kindred. Even your brother must bow down to you. Whoever curses you, may he be cursed; and blessings fall on him who blesses you. For you are my first-born son and my heir, and you have gladdened your father's heart."

Isaac stopped speaking, and a moment later Jacob came out of the tent. His face was deathly pale and covered with sweat, and he shook from head to foot so that he could scarcely strip off the pieces of goatskin and Rebecca had to help him.

"Come away from the tent flap!" she whispered, half pulling, half leading him out of earshot. When they were far enough from Isaac, she grasped Jacob's arms and shook him.

"What is it, what's the matter?"

He did not speak or look at her, and when she went on pleading with him, he tore the last bit of goat hide off his neck, threw it at her feet, and, pulling away from her, ran off stumblingly to his own tent. When she followed him there, she found him lying on the ground, with Esau's borrowed clothes strewn around him. His face was hidden in his arms, but he still trembled wildly and his shoulders rose and fell as if with sobs.

"My son—" she said, kneeling beside him. "It is all over. He believed you. You have the blessing and none can take it from you now."

"I know it," said Jacob brokenly. "Oh, leave me! I must think. I must try to understand what I've done."

At that moment they both heard Esau returning from the hunt. He passed the tent and they heard him building up the fire. Then he called one of his wives to help him.

"I must take back the raiment!" muttered Rebecca.

She gathered the scattered clothes together and hurried back with them to Esau's tent. The other wife, Judith, was picking over lentils in a corner, and looked up at Rebecca as she came in.

"Why did you take my lord's clothes?" she asked.

"I took them to mend, since you are too idle or not skilled enough," Rebecca retorted. "Say nothing to him or he will be angry that his mother must still tend him." The girl glanced at the clothes, then back at Rebecca. Even in her dull eyes, there shone the gleam of realization that this, at least, was a lie; but she dared not say anything. And almost at once, before Rebecca could leave, Esau strode into his tent.

He stopped. "Mother?" he said. "What is it?"

"I have prepared your clothes for you, my son," she said. "This raiment is most suitable for you to take food to your father."

"Thank you," he said, staring at her. Rebecca felt herself grow hot. Was it shame? She would not let herself succumb to it. She withdrew from the tent and went and sat with Jacob. They sat silently together for a long time; she stroked his hair and tried not to think what must be passing in Isaac's tent, nor to predict what would happen next. But of course it was not unexpected when Esau burst in, his red skin flushed a deep, choleric crimson, his eyes wild with anger like a bull's, but weeping as only a man can weep. Those frantic tears took away from him the look that would otherwise have been that of a rage-crazed beast, and the sight of them smote Rebecca's very soul, for in a flash she remembered how she had soothed his tears in childhood, how this one, too, was her son, and that she had defrauded him.

He stood in the tent mouth, holding the sides of the opening with his great hands; he swayed forward, dragging on the tent, which swayed and cracked on its poles.

"*You!*" he bellowed.

Jacob had started up at the sight of him, and stood lightly poised on both feet, crouched a little as if ready to run. Rebecca sprang up, too, and stood before him.

"The sin be upon me," she cried.

"Sin indeed, you false and treacherous woman!" roared Esau. "I leave you to God, or if He is against me too, then to your own thoughts. For you have often told me that you saw me being born, so who knows better than you who came first? For your fancy, for your vanity, because he flattered you, you have done this to me, who loved and respected you with as true a heart as that—that—"

Here he broke off and pointed, not a finger, but his whole huge red fist at Jacob.

"But you I will not leave to God. I don't trust God to

punish you! I shall do it. You got my birthright through my own folly as much as your cunning, but the blessing you got through wickedness and lies and cruel, cruel deceit! If you could see my father now, both of you, your greedy, false hearts would burst in your breasts for very shame! He trembles and weeps for what he has done, he sees Hell opening before him because he betrayed me all unwittingly and gave the blessing where it does not belong! Go to him, woman—I will not call you my mother any more. Go to your husband and see what a ruin you've brought about! Go, or I will carry you there on my back and fling you at his feet!"

Rebecca, distracted, rushed from the tent, but as she went she heard Esau say in dreadful tones of menace to Jacob, "You shall never enjoy the blessing. I am going to kill you now—I am going to tear the blessing out of you, for it was *stolen—stolen—stolen!*" She was paralyzed to hear the sound of blows, and then almost at once Jacob came fleeing out of the tent, bent over, protecting his head with both arms. She caught his hand, quick as thought, and led him into Isaac's tent.

The old man lay half insensible on his back, rolling his eyes and uttering deep groans. He did not seem to know them. They heard Esau blundering about outside, cursing and raving, and then he came bursting in. Rebecca, terrified as she was, jumped into his path as he reached for Jacob.

"Stop!" she cried. "Whatever *we* have done, you will not take revenge here, in your father's tent, while he lies perhaps on his deathbed?"

The great bullish figure of Esau hung over her for a moment, and then seemed to shrink down. His arms dropped to his sides, his head bowed; his shoulders were heaving, and the breath gurgled in his throat. After a while he said in a growl, "No, I will not defile my father's tent as you have. Let the old man die in as much peace as you have left him. I won't add to his misery." The massive shaggy head came up and he glared at Jacob. "But hear me, brother! One part of the blessing at least I have power to cancel, for I shall never serve you, never. And if you wish to live, see to it that you are far from here before our father dies; for when he has left the world, no more restraint shall keep me from your throat. For that woman"—he pointed to Rebecca, who shrank back in horror from the hatred in his eyes—"has no more power or influence over me, and if I must do without my father's blessing, so she must do without her elder son's."

The impact of these words on Rebecca was crippling. She felt them as a mortal blow, but it did not immediately incapacitate her. Waiting numbly till Esau had gone, she drew Jacob to her, controlling both his trembling and her own by keeping an iron grip on his arm.

"What have we done, Mother?" asked Jacob, suddenly childish, staring in awe and agitation at his father.

"We have done what we have done," she said, and her voice was clipped and cold though she burned to shed tears and break into wails. "We must still believe it is for the best. Nothing will be helped if you die. I will help you to get ready, and you must then ride off at once, for your father may not live through the night. By morning you must be far away."

"But where? Where shall I go?"

"You must go to Aram, to my kinsmen," she said. "Tell my brother Laban, if he still lives, that you are your father's heir, and that your mother entreats him to take care of you until I send for you to return. Don't look so broken, Jacob," she added. "While you are there, let my brother look about for a wife for you—a good wife, from among our own people. She will comfort you. But beware of my brother, for he is greedy and dishonest." Mother and son looked in each other's faces, remembering that, in the eyes of Esau, they were no better. Then they flung themselves on each other's necks. Rebecca still kept her feelings reined in, but Jacob, usually so reserved, let his emotions burst out of him like a flashflood roaring in torrents down a dry wadi. Rebecca held him in her arms till the storm passed, knowing that her own grief, her own terrible, lifelong doubt, and the pain of the wound Esau had given her were yet to begin.

Three

Leah and Rachel

I am Leah, daughter of Laban of Padan-Aram, wife of Jacob called Israel. And I am the mother of sons.

I am old now. Looking back on my long life, it seems to me that the only *pure* happiness I have known ended with the birth of my sister Rachel when I was eight years old. It may seem odd that I still, in my age, remember that lovely time of childhood so clearly. I cannot remember what happened a few days ago, and yet those memories are as bright in my heart as newly fused glass.

My father was a strange man, and (now I can say it) not a good one, but me he loved as none has loved me since. This was not to be looked for, since I was a female child when he, of course, wanted a son; yet I'm told he looked at me, in his natural disappointment, and something in my eyes untied the bitter knot in his breast and warmed him to me.

"She has the eyes of a young doe," he said. "We will call her Leah"—which is a gazelle.

The Lord knows, I have no reason for vanity; yet none can say that my eyes have no beauty. But alas, those eyes, which won the hard heart of my father Laban, did not perform their function as less beautiful eyes do. To see them (my father said) was to rejoice; but to see *through* them was a trial and a hardship, for they were partly blind, and are now entirely so.

Still, as a little girl I knew and cared nothing for my weak sight. It spared me the knowledge that in all other features I was plain, as plain as a she-goat. My first knowledge of this was long delayed, for my parents loved and petted me as long as I was their sole darling. My father brought me the new lambs to caress and all the flowers of the fields to smell in spring; in the time of harvest, the most delicate first fruits were always for me. My nose, my tongue, and my quick fingers did the work of my eyes so that I hardly realized that others saw more than the dim moving shapes, the glancing lights, and the quiet shadows that were all my visible world.

Through this world I played and danced and sang with all my heart. I knew the fullness of love, both given and received. I learned to help my mother in the work of women about our tent, relishing the shiny feel of the grains running through my fingers, the heavy texture of the dough as I dug my fists into it, the swish of the broom and the prickly smell of dust as my mother swept the threshing floor. I learned to avoid burning myself and yet to enjoy the kindly warmth of the fire when nights were cold, and to call my mother when the good smell of roasting meat or baking bread began to turn into the acrid smell of burning. All these scents and sensations became my small daily joys.

The greatest of these was when my father would gather me on his knees at the end of the day, and I would smell the strong satisfying smell of the sheep and sheep's milk on his robe, mingled with his own male smell—the smell peculiar to him and, so, beloved—and feel his rough, tickling beard as he kissed my face. My world was beautiful and blessed, though at the time I thought it all quite natural and felt no special gratitude. Later I learned how favored I was, and had cause to wonder if God did not purposely cram a whole lifetime's happiness into those eight short years, as one who says, "There is your portion. Be content."

Then Rachel came.

My mother, who had given up hope of more children, was half mad with delight when she found she had again conceived, and of course my father's hopes of an heir were renewed. I often wonder what my life would have been had Rachel been a boy. But Rachel was Rachel: small, delicate, and lovely, where I was clumsy and ill-made. . . . At first I did not know this, for I could not see her well and had never seen myself; but it was not long before I got hints from others that my sister in some mysterious way outshone me, even though she was just a little toddling thing while I was a grown girl of ten.

As for my father, I will not say he changed toward me, for, strangely enough, I remained his favorite (as I later discovered by his actions on my behalf); but no father, deprived of sons, could help taking pride and pleasure in so beautiful a substitute as Rachel was. While he loved me in a deep, simple way, upon her he doted; and my mother, seeing her own faded beauty repeated and begun anew, could not help clucking and cooing and talking constantly of Rachel's sweet face and graceful body, her curly hair and small dainty hands and feet, until I would run from her side and hide behind the well so that I might cry out my jealousy and bewilderment in peace.

One day I was there when some of my father's people came to water their beasts. They were young men, avid for wives, and they were talking of the girls in the village, comparing them. They did not mention Rachel at first, for she was still a child; but I was then twelve and old enough to be considered.

After listening to them discussing this one and that, a strange, tense dread came over me when one of them said, "Of course, there is Leah, of Laban." There followed a silence and the same man heaved a sigh. "It is a pity. . . . She has the hips of one who will bear easily, and her father is quite well-to-do-now. Her portion will be large."

"The more so since he must be anxious to get her off his hands," said another with a laugh.

"Yes, the dowry for an ugly elder daughter must always be higher than for a pretty younger one," said a third. "For myself, I might take Leah, for all her lack of beauty; but who wants a weak-eyed wife? One would have to do half her work, or wed another just for that purpose. And the worst of it is, her bad sight may be passed to her children."

"It would be too bad," said the first, "if your sons, Nathan, had her weak eyes and your weak head." They all laughed, and the one they joked at retorted, "From both of us they might still inherit strong backs! Nevertheless I don't want ill-favored children."

"Then you must wait and marry her sister Rachel, for it will take a double portion of beauty in the mother to outweigh the ugliness of the father," mocked the voice of the first young man, as they rounded up their flocks and drove them back to the village.

When they had gone and all was quiet again, I crept from my hiding place and drew up water from the well in the leather bucket. Setting the bucket down where the light fell on it, I hung over it, begging the spirit of the well to show me my face. I had tried before, but never so hard. I rubbed my eyes, as this sometimes helped a little to clear away the perpetual mist; but all I could make out was a wavering shape full of glimmering points of light. My eyes I could just see—two dark, oval pools within the pool; tears fell out of them and broke up the image into ripples which I could see only as interlocking circles of light.

I walked home. My mother was working. I wanted to speak to her, to ask her about what the men had said; but she was busy and out of temper. Patiently I waited until my father returned, and, when I had served him and he had eaten, I crept up to him and leaned against his side.

"Father, am I very ugly?" I asked.

He started, and then put his arm around me.

"Your eyes are the most beautiful in the village," he said.

"But are they wasted, where they are?"

"Daughter, these thoughts will only make you sad. A woman must not be judged by her looks, but by her virtues. And of these you have many."

"But no matter how good and patient I try to be, it will be no use if—"

"If what?"

"If for any reason no man will want to marry me."

I hoped he would laugh, as he often had when I was younger, laughed away my fancies and called them nonsense. But he didn't laugh. He only held me close and said, in a tone which told me he was holding his teeth hard together, "I tell you one thing, little doe. Marry you shall, that I promise you. For you are worth ten of these idle, worthless, sniggering village harlots with their bold eyes and their light ways. A little persuasion may be needed, for young men are fools, empty of judgment; but when you are safely wed, your husband will come to me and say, 'Father Laban, may the gods bless you for your wisdom and generosity, in giving me a wife without equal.' Meantime, daughter, look to it that you learn all the duties of a wife, in so far as you can; for it is true that your weak eyes are a disadvantage, and you must strive to make up for it. Leave the rest to me and shed no more tears, for they spoil these dear, tender eyes that I love." And he kissed them, and sent me off comforted—for the time.

But as Rachel grew, her loveliness blossomed, till all the village seemed to be speaking about it. The kindness of many prevented their mentioning it before me; but there was no impediment to my hearing, and I often heard more than was meant for me. It was not that I did not love her, for sisters must love each other, and she could be good to me at times—she could afford it; but in my heart I could not help knowing that she had in her nature a measure of slyness and deceit that was not in me. She had no patience, and she was, moreover, often lazy, as (I have learned) many beautiful women are, knowing that their beauty is enough—just as I knew that my lack of it made hard work and other virtues all the more necessary.

Another fault she had, which is common to many girls who have more than their fair share of beauty. As she ripened, her eyes turned more and more toward men, and when the men returned her looks she did not drop her eyes, but used them cunningly to enslave the men to her. This I knew through hearing the young men talk, and some of them grew wild with love for her. Little my sister cared for the suffering she caused, and fortunate it was for her that my parents kept her close, or she might have shared the fate that, years later, overtook my own daughter Dinah. But this I must tell in its place (if indeed I can bear to).

Maidens of our tribe could be married at ten, and, as I've said, many wanted my sister and vied with each other to have her, yet none had ever asked for me. There was one young man whom my sister liked, and she plagued our father to let her go to him, but he refused and refused until even our mother (who had recently conceived again, past the years of expectation, and was caught between fractiousness and joy) begged him to make peace in the house by letting her have her way. But my father said angrily:

"No! I will not suffer my little first-born to dance at the wedding of her sister till she is herself a bride. She has enough to bear. Leave plaguing me, both of you, for my word is said on the matter."

So Rachel sulked awhile, and the young man left the village, and the rest went on gazing and hoping. And then *he* came.

It happened early one morning, when I was twenty and Rachel in her thirteenth year. She had gone out with the sheep, for my father was unwell and my mother was tending him. I was at home, too, for I now had two little brothers, one only a few weeks old and the other nearly two years, who both loved me and whom I loved like my own children. My mother was far from young and had not my patience with them, so I had charge of them much of the time, and a glad charge it was, though spoiled sometimes by the secret fear that they were all the sons I would ever have.

Suddenly in ran my sister, breathless and trembling, and flung herself down beside my father where he lay on his couch.

"One has come, Father!" she cried, panting. "His name is Jacob and he is the son of my aunt Rebecca whom you've often told us of. He is his father's heir and, moreover, both young and handsome!"

"Softly, my ewe," said Father (for such is the meaning of her name). "Young and handsome the youth may be, but if he claims to be his father's heir he has a false tongue. His brother Esau came into the world before him, though only by a little." But Rachel would not be interrupted.

"Father, he could not lie, not he! When you see his eyes, you will know! Let me tell you of him quickly, for he is coming now—I ran on ahead to warn you. Listen. You know the great stone that covers the southern well? That it takes three men to roll away? Well, when Jacob saw me, coming down with the sheep, he leaped up, all trembling, and tears came into his eyes as I approached him, and suddenly when I was close beside him, looking up curiously—for I've never seen a man weep so before—he turned very suddenly to the well and, with a great effort, rolled away the stone all by himself, so that the other shepherds there gave a cry of surprise at his strength. Then all the flocks rushed to drink, so that we two stood there like two trees with the sheep jostling and flowing past us, pressing us together, and he said to me, 'I am Jacob, son of

Isaac and Rebecca. Who are you?' And when I told him, he threw his head back and clenched his fists, thus, and cried out to the sky, 'Is this then the heaven that was at the top of the ladder? And am I not now unworthy of it?' And then he kissed me, calling me his little cousin. What did he mean, do you think, Father?"

"Nay, how can I know, Rachel? Perhaps he will explain. Come, wife, help me up, for ill or well I must welcome my sister's son."

But Jacob came in before he could robe himself, and I could see his figure was tall and his shoulders broad and that his hair and beard gave his head a fine, kingly shape. Also his voice was gentle, especially in speaking to the little boys, which warmed me to him.

But it soon became clear that the madness Rachel inflicted upon so many young men she had bestowed on her cousin in even heavier measure, so that he could scarcely bear to be out of her sight. His voice shook and thrilled with tears whenever he spoke to her, and sometimes it altogether failed him, so that I had to give him a little push to get him started, for he would simply gaze speechlessly at her as at some spirit. But I fought down my jealousy, and indeed it was easier by this time because I was used to the annoying proofs of love shown by nearly every man who came near her. I thought, in my folly, that Jacob was just one more of these, and my father's promise armed me to bear another worshiper.

I understood from their talk that he was only visiting us because of some trouble he had had with his brother, and that soon his mother would send for him. In the meantime he worked for my father with the sheep.

Rachel, who was in a fever of excitement about him and who sang his praises to me as often as we were alone, told me that his handling of the flocks was most expert and that his gentleness with them was producing an almost miraculous increase of milk. It was the lambing season, and

Rachel related that, when Jacob tended the flock, there was not one stillborn, and that there were so many twin births that our father could not believe his good fortune.

"That is because Jacob is a twin himself," Rachel solemnly explained. "Also his God is very powerful, though He is only one. Jacob has told me all about his God, and I am going to serve Him too, if Father will let me. Not that he could stop me if—"

"If what?" I asked her, although I knew.

"Leah, I love him! No, this time I am sure, don't tease me for I am all open to pain, and you—you are all kindness and goodness. Oh, I wish I were like you! Why am I not good and patient and industrious as well as beautiful? Only then would I be worthy of him! Yet he loves me, though I am not good enough. I know it, I know it! And soon he will ask for me, and this time Father shall not refuse, for if he does I shall die!"

"He will not let you marry before me," I said in my plain, heavy way which often maddened her.

Rachel, who had been clinging to me, jumped up in sudden anger, her voice changing.

"Oh, you are cruel!" she said. "You pretend to be good, but you are like a goat that stands in the doorway of a house and lets no one in, though it has no use for the house itself. Because none will marry you with your sheep's face and thick limbs, must I be denied love? Is it my fault you have no beauty? It is so unjust, I will not bear it!"

She tried to run away, but I reached out like a snake and caught her skirts, holding them fast so that she nearly fell. Bitterness came up into my mouth, but I spoke quietly.

"It is you who are cruel. I am not the goat you speak of, who bars the way into a house that it does not need. Am I not a woman? Might I not desire Jacob as much as you?"

"You?" she cried, her voice shooting upward, sharp as

an arrow shot at a quail. "You can't even see his face! Any man would do for you, and for my part I pray every day to every god there is that someone, anyone will come and wed you. But Jacob is not for you, sister, so kill your hopes at once. You are too old, too plain, and too blind, and, besides, *he is mine!*"

She twitched her garment from my hand and was gone like a desert whirlwind, leaving me shaking and ashamed. What had made me speak? And if at all, why these words? For I had never thought of Jacob as a husband—Rachel was right—he was far beyond anything I could hope for. Yet the words had come from somewhere, and now I knew they were true. I did want him.

Some days later my father came to me.

"Leah," he said. "I have news."

"It is no news to me," I said dully, for those days had been full of misery and dread. "Rachel is to marry Jacob." My father was silent. "Your word to me is broken," I said, beginning, against my will, to weep. "And I know well why! You could afford to send those village youths away disappointed, for in any case you felt they were unworthy of her, and brought you neither honor nor wealth. But Jacob, the heir of Isaac! Here is a match that neither you nor your word can withstand. But a word is a word, Father! No riches should have power to force it back in your throat. Am I not your first-born, and did you not love me?"

"I do love you, Leah, but—"

"Then spare me. Spare me this anguish! For she mocks me with my ugliness, and I have told her—I have told her—" my tears stifled my speech for a moment, but I forced myself on. "In a moment of anger I said a true word that I regret from my heart. I love him too, Father! And since that moment when I knew it, it has grown and grown, until now it rules me. To see her married before me would have been hard, but to him—that is beyond what I can bear!"

I flung myself on his neck and he held me until my weeping stopped. Then he said, quietly and yet with a sort of anger in his voice, "Leah, I could not know, when my word went from me, that Jacob would come here. In any case it begins to seem to me that my word was foolish, for I now see that it could mean two unmarried daughters instead of one. No," he said as I began to weep afresh, "don't weep, but listen to me. I cannot for my honor refuse him. But I will make him work for her for seven years. In such a time much can happen. I will strive to find you a good husband meanwhile, and if I fail—well, in seven years even one as slow in wits as your father may think of something. So be comforted, for your trial is delayed, and may never come."

Those seven years were to me a mixture of joy and misery. It was joy to live near him, to see him every day, to cook his food and serve him; there was a kind of closeness in it—almost, in some ways, the closeness of marriage. He became fond of me. Not as he was of *her*, but with the fondness of a brother or a friend. Sometimes we would sit in the firelight at evening and talk together, and once he said, "Leah, why must you be so understanding?"

Though his words were kind, his tone was dissatisfied. I carried these words away with me to my corner and lay with them, and next day they were still with me. What was their meaning? I searched for it for three days, and at last I found it—I found it by hearing a snatch of their talk.

They were not quarreling—they never quarreled as most people quarrel, with shouts and curses and blows, but sometimes, as the years wore on, it became hard for them to wait in chastity for each other and their meetings became stressful.

Rachel was asking him for one of the little glass bottles of skin oil that could be bought from a traveling merchant. Jacob said that, though he loved her and wanted to give her presents, he was only a hired laborer to our father, who, on the excuse of their being related, paid him very little.

"But you said you were your father's heir, and that you left him on his deathbed!" Rachel said. "Did you lie to me? My father says your brother Esau is older than you. If you spoke truly, then why are you so poor?"

Jacob hesitated, then answered that there were things he could not explain. "Yet I can tell you that I am the heir, when my father dies—for strangely, he lives on; but I can't go home to claim my inheritance. My mother's messages warn me to stay away. My brother has sons growing up, while I have none to stand with me."

Rachel began grumbling, but Jacob kissed her quickly (out of sight of my father) and said, "When we are married I will give you all you could wish for. I am skilled with the flocks; your father already owes me a third of his wealth in stock that would have died, or not been born, but for me. Patience! Borrow a little from your sister's store of understanding and pity me, for these years are hard for me, Rachel."

Borrow from *my* store . . . I understood. He would not have wished me, poor, plain Leah, to show more of any good quality than his beloved. . . . I threw away the words I had cherished and for days kept my eyes away from him, my ears closed to his voice. I tried to deaden my heart. But it was no use. He was there, always there . . . his special calls to the sheep had power to thrill me when I heard them across the sand at sunset, or woke to them at dawn; the smell of him, the sudden blessed coolness as his shadow fell on me unexpectedly as I crouched by the baking stones. . . . There was no escape from my love, or from the knowledge that it was fated to come to grief.

At that time I would have married any man, no matter how old, how poor; I would have married a leper and been grateful to tend his sores till I died beside him of the same dreadful disease, if only I could have escaped the day that was coming, the day when Jacob's bondage would be ended and he would marry my sister and carry her to his tent. . . . Once when I was beside the well, I looked into its depths. I saw nothing; but the very breath from my mouth made a hollow tremor within the deep stone cistern. The midday sun was scorching my back and yet my face was cool, and so were my arms when I reached them in. . . . A little further, and down I would drop, like the pebbles my brothers would toss in, calling the names as they fell to see who would end up in the well: "Fa-ther, Mo-ther, Le-ah, Ra-". But the faint splash would always come at my name, and they would shout, "Leah, Leah! It's you again!" Perhaps it would be a kinder fate than that which awaited me. . . . Yet I drew back my arms into the blaze of noon, and carried my full jar home as if I had not been very close to death, regretting my cowardice even while I rejoiced that I was still alive. . . .

The night before the wedding I was too busy to suffer much. My mother and I ran to and fro preparing food and lodging for the guests who would crowd our house tomorrow. I questioned myself. I seemed so strong and calm; could I continue so, or would all fortitude forsake me the next day, allowing me to weep or scream or run away as I so often had in my dreams? No, I was sure I would not. Was it that I loved him less, was my envy of her less sharp? No. It was only that time had accustomed me to the idea. If one had seven years to look forward to an agonizing death, when the time came one would have lived through its terrors so many times in imagination that the reality might seem almost tolerable.

Long after Rachel had gone to her rest and even my mother had crept into her corner and pulled the skins over her, I was still at work, for I was afraid to lie down and try to sleep. When there was nothing more for me to do I went out under the stars. They were almost as thick as the sands of the desert; or so they seemed to me—a hazy, bright mist above my head with only one or two standing clear. But the night air was as cool and as sweet as well water, and I breathed it in, and suddenly I found myself timidly offering a prayer, not to one of our own gods, but to the God Rachel talked of, Jacob's God.

"God of my sister's betrothed," I began. "None else can help me. I have done all my best, these seven years; for every drop of Jacob's sweat, I have spilled a tear, and yet none have known but You—if indeed You know all, as they say. Therefore, since before me lies what I cannot bear, either let me die now, in the shadows of this peaceful night, or somehow numb my soul that I may not feel the keenness of pain when they are joined."

I felt a quietness descend on me, but I could not be sure if it meant my prayer was heard, or simply that I was at last ready for sleep. I turned to go back into the house and then leaped backward with a gasp. A tall dark shape stood behind me. It was my father.

"Leah," he said. "The time is here. How is your love for Jacob, that you once told me of? Have the years worn it away?"

"No, Father. But let us not speak of it, for I can't bear it unless it is kept hidden."

"Leah," he said again, "I have thought much of what you said. A word is a word, and I gave my word to you, did I not? I swore an oath that you would be married first. That was my first word, before I gave one to Jacob. No man has come for you, despite all I have done, so I must ask—which of my words must I keep, the one to you or the one to Jacob? Which has precedence, that is what I ask myself. Why, the one to my elder daughter has precedence, surely, for I gave it first, and she is my own flesh.

Besides," he went on, as if arguing with himself, "why must I yield up my other daughter to a poor shepherd, or that poor shepherd, despite his skill, to my daughter? I reason thus: I will marry him first to you, and then, if he still wants *her*, I will keep the three of you for seven years more. My word to you will be kept, and my word to him only a little broken—a break which seven years will see mended. What say you, daughter?"

What could I say? I am not a clever woman; my brain serves me but slowly. I understood his words, yet could not grasp his intention, far less balance the good in it against the evil. One thing only was clear to me—he had said I was to marry Jacob. I! I! But how? That question, it seemed then, was all that concerned me; it was not for me to argue the right or wrong, especially when he added, "I have consulted my gods, and they are agreed. I am on the right course."

"Father—Father—it is not possible—is it?" I gasped, pressing my breast to keep my heart from leaping out of it.

"It is possible. After the feast tomorrow, you, and not Rachel, shall veil yourself and enter his tent. Be sure the light is out—that will seem to him no more than a maiden's modesty demands. Lie still, say nothing, and accept his love. Then you will be united and nothing can change it."

The rapture that came over me at this all but pre-vented any sensible thoughts about the matter, but as I began to imagine how it would be, I was at once brought up short by my reason.

"But, Father! When he feels my face he will know at once! My features are—coarse—where hers are fine. How will he not know me?"

"My child, not all fingers are as sensitive as yours. *You* would know *his* face from all others in the world, no doubt; but remember, he has never touched yours, and we have kept Rachel close. Perhaps he has stolen some tokens these past seven years, but her body is a stranger to him.

Also . . . Well, an eager bridegroom far gone in festal drinking, alone with his bride, does not trouble himself much about the size of her nose! Be at ease on that point; he will be deceived."

Deceived! The word made me shudder. It brought near to me, like a black cold shadow, knowledge of the wickedness of what we were about.

"But Father, what of the morning? What when he awakens and finds me, and not Rachel, at his side? Will he not be mad with anger, will he not turn me away, or at the least, hate me forever?"

My father embraced me. "You he could not hate, my doe. As to turning you away, he will not dare. I will take the blame, and soften it at once by promising him Rachel in addition. What man does not prefer two wives to one? He once told me when in wine that he wished the virtues of my two daughters were wrapped up in one. Well, now he will have you both—of what can he complain?"

"But Father, is it just, to make him work another seven years for Rachel?"

"He can think of it how he pleases, either that the past seven earned her and the next seven will earn you, or the other way around."

"For me he would not work even one year, past or future," I said. "Let the seven, which is a great length by any reckoning, content you for the two of us, and let him return to his own place."

"That he can't do, my dear," he returned promptly, and not without satisfaction. "I happen to know that his brother's anger against him is far from cooled, and until he has sons of his own to defend his claims, he dare not return. Besides, I must think of myself. Your brothers are growing, your mother is old and feeble now—we need our daughters to help us, and, I confess it, I would be lost in the fold without Jacob's skill. It is my right as his father-in-law to retain his service while I can. Come—you have worked hard, and your heart's pain has helped to tire you. You must go to bed, for tomorrow night you will sleep little!" He chuckled in the way men do about such matters, while a woman shrinks and wonders and trembles at what lies before her.

And so I spent the last night of my maidenhood wide awake, turning my father's scheme over and over in my head, trying to put my soul at peace by discovering somehow that it was right. I consulted the gods, all of them, even Jacob's; they were all dumb. I received no guidance but that of my own conscience on one hand and my own desires on the other. Yet it was all futile, for I was my father's chattel, grown woman of twenty-seven though I was, and must obey him. In that knowledge I rose in the morning and went about my work, concealing my violent feelings behind the veil I wore to hide me from the guests.

The day passed slowly, slowly, slowly. Rachel was like a lark, soaring and swooping and singing. . . . I watched her, my heart baffled within me. I had not thought of her. How would my father prevent her from impeding the plan? But that was not my concern. He would do it somehow. About her feelings, I dared not let myself think. I had enough to do to control my own. "I will take the blame," my father had said . . . Well, upon him be it! There are times when it is good to be a chattel. Chattels need not consider love or hate, right or wrong, loyalty or treason. They need only obey.

Night came at last. The feast was still going on, but Jacob rose and took his leave of the guests amid much laughter and joking. He was beautifully robed and his body was scented with oil. The scent of that oil, wafting to me as he brushed past where I was sitting on the ground, unnoticed, put a notion into my head. As a wedding gift he had given Rachel the perfume she had begged for; it stood now, in its glass flacon, beside her. He knew the smell of it, for she had waved it under his nose when he gave it to her, saying, "Only a breath now—later you will have your fill." (She had grown very bold with him in all the years of their betrothal.) Now I moved to her side. "It is time for you to go to your groom," I said. "Mother is waiting to prepare you." She jumped up gaily and ran off, forgetting the bottle, which I caught up and hid in my scarf. I saw my father rise too from among his guests and make his way through the merrymaking crowds, following Rachel. I did not let my thoughts follow *him*. . . . Carrying my prize, I made my way to my mother's room, and there made my own preparations.

Then I waited, seated on the floor. The scent of the stolen perfume was all about me. Beside me was a small lamp, its wick flickering in the last of the oil—soon it would go out. Soon, soon—I clenched my hands. My father stood suddenly before me.

"Come," he said.

I picked up the lamp. My hand did not tremble now. I followed him through the dark night, my little lamp one point of light through the mist of my imperfect sight. The sound of my father's footfalls led me. At the flap of Jacob's tent, he paused. The lamp flame died.

"It is a good omen," he said. "Get you in. Love him well and bear him sons, then you need fear nothing. Give me your hand . . . good, it is as steady as rock, and yet not half so cold. . . . In, in. He awaits you."

Then he was gone.

I entered. I could hear breathing. As Jacob saw my shadow move against the stars in the mouth of the tent, he started up.

"Rachel—Rachel—"

The sound of that name, spoken in his voice, so choked with joy and passion, passed through me like a spear. For a second I thought of us, her and me, as we were in that mo-

ment: myself, closed in his arms, ablaze with guilt and desire; Rachel, otherwise enclosed, her cries muffled (for,
chattel or not, *she* would not take it peaceably, not Rachel!)
while her guests still laughed and danced and feasted, and
her sister lost both maidenhead and honor in *her* marriage
tent.

My lord slept in tranquillity, but I lay awake with my fear,
my shame, and my love. I laid my hand upon him, thinking
that perhaps never again would he lie so at my side, in perfect contentment; as the dawn came and light crept
through the cracks in the tent, enough to show me to him
the moment his eyes should open, I wanted to jump up and
run, to find Rachel wherever she was imprisoned, release
her, force her to take my place . . . But to what purpose? I
was his wife, and nothing could change that. I lay quietly,
trying to still my fear, thinking, "Let him rather beat me in
his first rage of discovery, and love me later, than never
forgive me."

Soon after dawn my father looked into the tent.
When he saw me awake, he smiled at me, and showed by
gestures that he would be outside to prevent Jacob harm-
ing me. I was not consoled. It was his anger, not his brutal-
ity I feared. After such a night as I had passed, wrath in
my husband would be like a shadow upon the sun. Wretch
that I was, why had I been fated to buy my love at the cost
of so cruelly deceiving him? The thought cut so deep that
tears began to spill down my cheeks, and a sob broke from
me.

I felt a sudden sharp movement at my side, and, looking down, saw the dark pools of his eyes looking up at me.
He lay perfectly still for a long time. Then he started up,
in a short, violent movement, and sprang away from me,
staring at me as at some scorpion or serpent that, on wak-
ing, he had found curled at his side.

"Devils of hell!" he cried hoarsely. "I am cheated and abused! Where is your father? This is his doing, that I know, for you are too simple to be anything more than the false coin he has put into my hand! Oh, fool, fool, fool that I am! Why did I not heed my inner self? I knew! I knew it was not Rachel! I felt your coarse-grained body, your thin meager lips, even your clumsy hands. . . . Passion and wine deadened my wits. . . . Oh, to have been so deceived, so beguiled! God in heaven, is this the punishment I deserve?"

With these words he broke from the tent, bent over and staggering like a crippled beast, and went blundering and raving toward the house of my father. All his words were branded with fire on my memory, though at the time only a few pierced home; but, like the knife thrust which of many other stabs pierces the heart, they were enough. "Meager lips . . . clumsy hands . . ." And I had loved him all my best! I threw myself down where he had lain with me, clutching my head in my arms, and filled my mouth with the musty skins to keep from screaming, "Jacob! Jacob! Come back and kill me!" For I felt I could not live if, even for that one night, I had not pleased him. . . .

Something my father had said had made it quite clear to me that it was no part of his plan to give Rachel to Jacob before he had worked for a further seven years. I knew this—I am as sure of it now—because, buried in my heart had been the expectation of being Jacob's only wife during that time. In the moments of my worst fears about the plan, some little, secret voice within me had whispered, "A man cannot hate his only wife for seven years. He must turn somewhere for love, and if he is denied the woman he wants, he must grow to depend on the one he has." Perhaps the secret voice even slyly whispered, "He must grow to love her." For closeness between a man and woman can change them toward each other, just the closeness and no more. And thus I built upon a quicksand of hopes.

And very speedily did this give way and leave me to sink into despair. For on the very day after the marriage feast, my father began to yield. I watched it helplessly. Jacob did not do him actual harm—violence was not in his nature; but the force of his just rage was such that my father was afraid. At first, when Jacob had become a little more calm and was able to hear my father's words, he explained that his gods had forbidden him to break his word about me, that it was contrary to custom to give a younger daughter before an elder and that therefore he had imposed me upon Jacob as the only solution to his dilemma. With much hand spreading, many honeyed words, and not a few false tears, my father craved pardon if he had wronged him, but vowed that all would be put right. Rachel should indeed be his; but—and here he already began to falter—a further period of service would be necessary, since she was his only remaining prop, the darling of his aging heart . . . and thus, and so, all in that singsong, whining tone he used in bargaining over a camel or a sack of grain in the market, when he was getting the worst of it with some sharp-eyed merchant. It was almost more than I could endure to hear him speak in that way to my husband, although I was never mentioned; the "merchandise" was Rachel—Jacob's tears, his moans, his furious pleas and demands were all for her.

And she? I went seeking her, lest she should come seeking me, and I found her where I had half expected, in the house of a wily, detestable relative on the other side of the village. He was the only man I could think of who would accept my father's bribe, do his bidding, and ask no questions. . . . I believe he would have thrown Rachel down the well for enough sheep and goats.

Indeed, when I saw her, she was in such a pitiful condition that one might have thought her a step away from death. I think she had not stopped weeping and wailing from the moment my father had laid hands on her the night before. Her garments were rent, her hair also; she had rubbed her face in the dirt and ground more into her flesh. The sight of my beautiful sister in such a state struck me dumb and stupid with shame, for she was lying on the floor like an animal, exhausted with grief, filthy and disheveled. I knew then that I loved her despite my jealousy, and remembered how I had played with her and nursed her when she was a baby; I felt how I had wronged her, though I did not know how I might have avoided it. . . . In a spasm of pity, and not only for her but for myself also, I lay down beside her and drew her into my arms.

She started, and I think would have repelled me when she saw who it was, but the poor thing was so weary after her long night of grief that any comfort, even from me, was precious. She began to weep afresh, moaning, "Wretch! False sister . . ." But she had no heart to abuse me, for she knew that, however I might have fallen in willingly with our father's scheme, at bottom it was not my fault, but his. So she clung to me like a child and I petted and comforted her as well as I could; how strange it was then, and how much stranger it seemed later, that at that of all moments we should feel so close to each other! And I am thankful for that hour; thankful that I had courage to seek her, kindness to pity her, strength to give her comfort and to raise and bring her home, wash her, dry her tears, change her garments, and restore her to herself; for no such moment of truly sisterly warmth ever happened between us again, till near the very end of her life.

The greatest restorative I could offer her, of course, was the news that Jacob was demanding that she be given to him at once, as soon as the week of feasting for *our* marriage was decently over, and that I foresaw that our father would be overruled by Jacob and consent, though such had not been his wish.

"He could not, he *could not* have expected us to wait seven long years more!" cried Rachel. "Oh, Leah, what did the gods mean by giving us such a man to be our father! His ruthless greed and dishonesty is our shame, too. Oh, he must consent, he must! If he does not, Jacob and I will fly from here, even though he has nothing!" Suddenly she stopped, thought, and then turned, gripping my shoulders. In her voice was a new timbre, that high note of rebellion and vitality that set her apart from me.

"Leah, listen! Why should we not go? No, but listen, Leah! I will seem patient, and submissive, and show no anger to my father. We will wait out the week, then, when we are both wed to Jacob, we will gather some of our possessions together secretly, take some camels and some flocks, and run from our father's house with our husband! Surely some such idea must have entered Jacob's head, too, for how could he bear to work a further period for our family after what has happened—especially if he has me already?" I stared at her, and shook my head.

"He would pursue us. We would be thieves!"

"Thieves! Who speaks of stealing? Jacob would take what he has richly earned. My father is a man of wealth now, thanks to Jacob's skill with the herd and good husbandry. He has been paid but a tithe of what he deserves! Did Father give you a handmaiden for your marriage?" I nodded. "Good, that means I shall get one too—I'll choose Bilhah—she loves me and can be trusted. With them to help us we can surely manage."

I said nothing. I felt unable to join in such a reckless plan. I knew myself. What others decided for me, I would do; all I cared for now was to be with Jacob as much as was agreeable to him, hoping that he would do right by me, and that, little by little, despite Rachel's presence, I might earn his love. Whether this should happen here or elsewhere hardly mattered, though the thought of leaving my brothers was painful.

The week of celebrations passed and at once another began. My poor mother took to her bed and did not rise from it again; the excitement of both her daughters marrying within a month was too much for her, though she lived on for some time. This seemed to me an added reason for staying at home, for the shock of our departure and the uproar that must follow it would surely have killed her.

But in any case, it was not to be; for now that we were both married to Jacob, he was our lord, and his decision had to be final on such a matter; and it turned out that Rachel had mistaken him, for not only had he no idea of leaving my father, but when Rachel suggested it to him eagerly, he disappointed her by flatly refusing.

"But, husband!" Rachel cried. "How can you hesitate! If you fear for our courage, put it from you, for I am strong enough for anything when I am roused, and Leah has more quiet strength than I in some ways. We will gather together all that we have that's of any worth, and you can select your due from the flocks; we will leave in the night and by morning be far away."

"No," said Jacob flatly, "we will not go."

"But why? Why? I don't want to live here any longer! I hate my father for what he did. Do you not hate him?"

"My feelings for Laban are unimportant," he replied. "I am concerned with other matters. He may break his word if he wishes; his gods are false, so it is unlikely his honor should be trustworthy. But my God is the true God, and I have solved the riddle He set me seven years ago. I know now what He requires of me, and that I will do—that, and more. For the thing I long for, seven years, or seven times seven years of labor is only a trifling price."

"But you have me already!" cried Rachel in her childishness; but I had guessed he meant more than this.

"What was God's riddle?" I asked.

He gave me a look, perhaps the first I had had from

him since that first morning; it was not a look of love, but had perhaps a little of respect in it.

"I will tell you—both of you," he said. "You are my wives, and it is fitting that you should try to understand God's purpose for me."

We sat near him, and he said, "Before I came here, I did a great wrong. My mother led me to do it, and some blame attaches to her; yet not all, for I was full-grown and knew what I was about. I defrauded my brother out of his birthright; I deceived my father. For this reason I fled my home and my inheritance; for this reason I have never returned to claim what is mine, but have left my brother Esau to enjoy it, for in a way it is rightfully, though no longer lawfully, his. It is not only fear of his revenge, and his sons', that keeps me from home, but a knowledge that I do not deserve benefit for what I did, but rather punishment. God has made this clear to me several times.

"On the way here, I stopped to sleep in a valley of many stones, one of which I laid my head on. And while I slept, I had a strange dream. I dreamed of an endless ladder, its foot among the stones near where I lay and its top invisible among the clouds. Up and down this ladder passed male figures, shining with light, whom I knew to be God's messengers. What lay at the top of the ladder I could only guess at, but this I noticed, that those of God's people who were climbing upward showed joyful faces, while those descending seemed to weep. It must be, I thought, that this ladder leads to heaven and to God. The stony place where I lay was quite barren, and in my dream—perhaps also in reality—populated by snakes and other venomous, creeping things, so that it stood in my mind for death, danger, and evil, while at the top lay some unspeakable bliss.

"Then a figure descended the ladder who was the Lord of my father Himself, and He promised that the land where I lay should be given to me and my seed, which should be, He said, as the dust of the earth. He said more:

that He would be with me wherever I went, and would not leave me till all was accomplished that He intended for me. He did not accuse me, yet the stone under my head seemed to press upon my brain and I knew that there was some mystery to the ladder that was not open to me, but needed thought and time to solve.

"When I woke in the morning, I used the stone as a foundation for an altar. I spilled oil on the ground and called that desert place 'the House of God,' because God had been there with me in my dream. But it was only later, when I had left and gone on my way, that I noticed that the cold imprint of the stone which had been under my head did not go away. I could still feel it, pressing into me, like a charge, a reminder. . . ." He leaned toward us. "Feel my temple, there," he said. Each of us in turn touched the side of his forehead. "Is it not as cold as the head of a corpse? *I feel that stone there still.*"

We looked at each other. His skin had felt quite warm to my touch. I saw Rachel was also puzzled. It must, I thought, be a notion of his, a reflection of his guilt at what he had done.

"When I came here to this place, the first person I saw was you, Rachel, coming toward me with the sheep. I knew at once that I was fated to love you, and that the road to you would be long and hard, for to get you easily would be a reward and I had not merited such a blessing. Therefore it is only just that I should labor even for double the time that was first appointed, and I shall fulfill it, because I am paying not only for you. By living here in poverty and bondage to a man I despise, I am helping to wipe out the sin I committed against my brother and earn my right to my destiny."

After a long moment of silence, he added, "Though I felt outraged when I found out the deception Laban put upon me, I see now that that, too, was God's design for me. For I am to have many sons, and with but one wife, however beautiful and beloved, it might not be done in the time. Seven years, and then, I believe, God will summon me back to my own place. . . . And by then I must have all my sons about me. All my sons. . . ."

So we settled down, the three of us. Jacob labored for my father as before, and we four women—we two and our handmaids, Zilpah and Bilhah—labored for him and for our father too, for our mother did not live above two months.

Those who had said long ago that I looked fecund were not belied, for I conceived upon my wedding night, and nine months afterward bore my first son, whom I called Reuben.

This name simply means "See my son," and was a common name among us; but to me it had a deeper meaning. I felt that by giving me a son at once, God—Jacob's God, to whom I was now wholly turned—had shown that He had looked on me in my sorrow; and also, I wished Jacob to look upon our baby and, for his sake, forgive me and love me.

But no. True, he took pride in Reuben; but to him, he seemed only the first of many. He accepted him as part of what *must* come to him as part of God's purpose; but he did not love him as he would have done had he been Rachel's child, for the sole and simple reason that he did not love me.

Since that first night he had not lain with me, though he came sometimes to my tent in order to appear to be doing his duty by me and not keeping himself only for Rachel. But it was not till Reuben was three months old that he lay with me again, and then he made it clear that he did it for one purpose only—a purpose which was duly fulfilled, for soon another son was born to me, and this one I called Simeon.

I had begun to feel bitter in my deepest soul; for what

more could I do to be loved? Now there were two sons from me, and still Rachel, for all her extra portion of his love, had none; yet he doted on her, while from me he accepted all as his due and gave nothing.

The following year, and yet again the next, I gave birth to male children. My sons were growing up around me, strong, well favored, never ill, giving their father no cause for anything but joy and pride in them. True, I grew fatter, and looked old enough to be Rachel's mother, while she was still as young and lovely and fresh as ever. Yet was it fair that Jacob ran straight to her each evening on his return from work, brought her presents, saved for her the titbits off his dish, and did not seem to care whether she gave him children or not? Why indeed should he, when I was growing old in repeated pregnancies and labors? Several times a year I was granted his favors, but they made me feel like a ewe brought to a ram; that is all I was to him, and my heart shriveled up in me with sorrow and neglect. Only for my sons did I somehow keep warm and alive one corner of it, that I might give them kind nurture and not begin to hate them for their father's sake as I had once hoped he would love me for theirs.

All this time, however happy she might seem to be in the sunshine of our husband's love, Rachel pined and chafed ceaselessly in her childlessness. I held my sorrows in, and none knew of them; but Rachel was not able to bear hers alone. It galled her bitterly to see me growing ripe with child year after year, bearing healthy sons and rearing them under her eyes; she could not for her pride let me see her weeping with envy, nor did she ever rail before me or before Jacob. But to Bilhah, her handmaid, she confided all her grief, and Bilhah told Zilpah her friend, who reported all to me. I pitied Rachel; but this selfless, sisterly pity dropped into the well of my own miseries and drowned

there. I could not approach her, and we were thus, by en-
vying each what the other had, denied the solace of mutual
consolation.

After the birth of my fourth son, Judah, God granted
me a little respite from bearing. When Jacob saw that I did
not conceive, he left me wholly to myself in the nights, not
coming to me even in token, but staying always with
Rachel. But none ever saw me weep. Zilpah, I'm sure,
thought me quite content, though I once overheard her
saying to Bilhah:

"If I were married, and my husband left me so much
to myself, I'm sure I should resent it! But perhaps the ways
of a man are not pleasing to my mistress."

And Bilhah, who was a lusty-looking girl, with broad
round hips and an overripe mouth, laughed heartily and
said, "That goes to show how unlike sisters can be, for
nothing is more pleasing to *my* lady!"

"Nor of less use to her, it would seem," returned Zilpah. "To my view, the cause is that she clings to the old
gods, instead of bowing down before the one true God of
her husband, as I and my mistress now do."

"Do you think it is that?" asked Bilhah. "If you are
right, that should mean, if our master lay with me, I, too,
would prove barren, since I believe in the old gods still."

"And doubtless you'd like to put it to the test," said
my handmaid. "But your mistress will never give you to
our master, loving-jealous of him as she is, you will see."

But Zilpah was wrong in this, for quite soon after this
conversation I was witness to another. (It should not be
thought I pried and listened, but our tent walls were thin
and they had no care to lower their voices, so I could
hardly help overhearing.)

The two girls were outside preparing the evening meal,
and Bilhah was singing. Zilpah, who was a more taciturn
and even sour-mouthed wench, told her to leave off, asking
what she had to be so happy about.

Bilhah quickly crouched beside her and said, "Who would not be happy! And I have you to thank, in part, or so I suppose; for it was you who told me I could never bear our master's children until I changed my beliefs, so I did. I left off worshiping the old gods and began to pray to yours. And see what has happened! Some nights ago, my mistress, as she lay with our lord, began to weep and groan, and told him to give her children or she would die. And for once he was impatient with her, and asked if she thought he was God Himself that he could make her fruitful. So she was silent for a while, and then she said, "There is another way. I'll give you Bilhah, and if she gives birth, I shall be her midwife; her son I shall adopt, and it will be like my own, and through her I shall have descendants." And it is to be so! Whether I've conceived or not, I can't tell yet, but before long I shall know. I never dreamed of such an honor!"

"That's a lie," said Zilpah, and I was surprised at her sharpness. "You've dreamed of little else. Well, I wish you joy, as much as you are worthy of." Then she left her and came inside the tent, and tried to hide her tears, but she couldn't, and after a while I went to her and embraced her and said, "I understand you. Don't weep. Your own course is not yet run; who knows what God may have in store for *you*, who deserve at least as much as Bilhah?" She looked at me quickly, dried her eyes, and said no more, but both our minds were busy.

I've no doubt it cost Rachel very dear to do what she did, but it would not hurt me in the least to give Zilpah to Jacob. It would gain me respect with him, deprive me of nothing, and add sons to my name without the travail of bearing them. However, I bided time, to see what would be the outcome with Bilhah. Sure enough, in due course she grew big and at the winter's end gave birth to a boy. When her time came, we all attended her, but Rachel did more—she sat upon the two birth stones herself, and cried, and groaned, and sweated more than Bilhah; and when the moment of birth was at hand, Zilpah and I lifted Bilhah up and sat her on Rachel's knees, so that the baby was born between them, and I, on my husband's orders, placed him, not in the arms of his natural mother, but in my sister's.

She looked down at him. Her face was puzzled, as if she were not sure what she ought to feel; for however she had tried to experience the birth pangs, in truth she had experienced nothing but the shadow of them. Though this was a custom among us, and did indeed give her rights upon the child, I myself never truly felt that it belonged to any but her who had borne him. For only the pains herald in the rush of love that naturally follows. And besides, can milk flow from dry breasts? Before long, Bilhah had of necessity to claim him back, and while he sucked life from her, he was hers alone. To her face came the true look of motherhood.

It was not her right to name him, however; that Rachel did, calling him Dan, and Bilhah's next child also she named, and he was Naphtali. After that, Bilhah had no more children. And, since Jacob's hunger for sons was not yet appeased, I made good my secret intention and gave Zilpah to him. Now he had four wives, and, before long, seven sons, and then we both—Rachel and I—said to him that his time was up with our father, for we were heartily sick of living near him now our mother was gone and our brothers grown to manhood. We longed for our own place where Jacob would be master and we might feel that we were wives and the mistresses of our homes, not mere daughters and chattels of our father.

But Jacob wouldn't heed us.

"Not yet, not yet. It is not yet time. When I have all my sons about me, then God will grant me a sign."

"Ask Father at least to give you your own flocks! At least build us our own house, so that we need no longer live in tents on the fringes of the town!" Rachel begged.

But Jacob refused, saying that his debt was not yet paid. "The ladder in my dream was steep and had many rungs," he said. "I may, for all I know, be only halfway up to my reward. When God is satisfied with me, He will tell me."

So we had to stay. Rachel grumbled much, but I was silent, for I had my four fine sons to tend, together with Gad, Zilpah's boy. And soon she bore another, whom I named Asher, which means "happy"—and I was, in my way, for the desires and sorrows of my youth were passing, as I thought, and I felt less lonely and despised than before. Reuben, my eldest, was eight years old now, sturdy and beautiful, as was Simeon, though he was more fierce in his behavior than I could have wished; he was quick to react to the slightest insult and would fight boys twice his age with a reckless ferocity that astonished me.

"He is like my brother," Jacob would say, shaking his head. "Even so would he fall on his enemies. . . ." I think he still feared Esau in his heart, and I even wondered if he might be delaying our departure as much from that cause as out of care for his soul.

My three other sons, Reuben, Levi, and Judah, would, I think, have been more gentle (for God knows neither of their parents were fighters!) but Simeon's ways influenced them. They looked upon him as their leader and dreaded his mockery, which he offered freely if they hung back. So they became young warriors all. Their wildness and ruthlessness displeased me, yet I could not avoid feeling proud as I watched their strength growing upon them.

Nevertheless, when Judah was five, and already evading me to chase after his brothers on their escapades, my tent began to feel empty by day, and my arms also. I was still in the time of life to bear, though not for much longer, and Zilpah, seeing my restlessness and perceiving its cause, one day advised me to tempt my lord back to me again in the hope of more sons; for none had been born to him since Asher.

"But what if I tempt him and then cannot conceive?" I asked.

"Mistress, do you not know of the fruit which helps a woman to conceive?" she asked. "It is the fig. Let one of your sons go into the far fields and bring you some." I was doubtful, but I asked Reuben to go for me, and after two hours he came back with his headcloth heavy with ripe figs.

Rachel came to the mouth of her tent and saw him coming.

"What is he bringing?" she asked.

"Figs," I answered.

Her face brightened.

"Figs! Are the figs ripe so early?" And without my leave she called to him. "Reuben! Be a good boy and give me some of your figs."

"They're for my mother," he said.

"Oh, she doesn't mind. Here, pour them into my scarf."

But something broke in me and I said, with a knife in my voice, "Take them into my tent." He went at once, with a frightened look.

"Why may I not have some?" Rachel asked peevishly.

"Send one of your own to fetch them for you," I said, surprised at myself.

"What do you mean? You know the children of my tent are too young. Share your figs with me, for, as I have heard, they are good medicine."

"What afflicts you?"

She stared at me. "You are cruel," she said slowly at last.

"Why do you say that? I only want you to understand that my son brings figs to me, not to you, and that you have no right to any of them. My tent is full of hungry young mouths; I need all I have."

"Give me but a handful."

"No."

"But Leah! This is not like you. All I ask is—"

"A share of what is mine? That is all I have ever asked of you, but I have not had it. Would you think it right to take all my figs? Yet the husband we were to share has been all yours."

"Ah! So that's it."

There was silence between us.

"Good," she said. "At last we have it before us. So here is what I shall do. Give me some of the figs, and say a prayer over them to the God of women Who blesses you with a son each time Jacob comes to you. In exchange, I will send him to you whenever you wish, until you again conceive. After that I shall have no power to withstand him."

"Tonight?"

"Tonight, and whenever you will, until you conceive."

"How can you do this?"

"I can do as I will with him. That is not your concern. Give me the figs, and bless them. If the gods will it, we shall both have sons."

Whether it was some bodily effect of the figs, as Zilpah believed, or whether it was now God's will that Rachel should at last have a child, I cannot tell. Rachel said it was my blessing upon the figs, and she thanked me from her heart before any other thing, when I laid her little Joseph in her arms. My own fifth son, Issachar, had been born a week before, so that now Jacob had ten sons, and we both thought he would be satisfied and leave Aram at last, but still he would not.

Now that Rachel had Joseph she cared little for any-

thing else, and sent Jacob to me as before, so that the following summer I gave birth to Zebulun.

Now I was nearly forty years old, and my life, by the
best reckoning of women, was half over. I did not want to
pass another pregnancy—to say the truth, I feared it, for I
was fat and my back and legs were no longer strong. Six
births are not many, I know; many women of my age had
ten children or more. Yet it was enough for me. I had done
my duty, and I had done it without the solace of love from
my husband. Now I craved a stop to it all, and when
Rachel asked, when Zebulun was six months old, "Shall I
send Jacob to you again?" I replied, "No. Enough for me.
Let me alone with all that, I am done with it." And she
shrugged and accepted it.

But now came the strangest turn of all my life. For
Rachel, having born Joseph, had lost interest in the pleasures of love, and Jacob was bereft. True, he had our handmaidens to satisfy the needs of his flesh, but he cared nothing for them, and besides they did not conceive and he was
still lacking one son to make the twelve he had set his heart
on.

And so, at last, long after I had ceased to expect it, he
turned to me. And I—I no longer wanted him.

He came to my tent one night when I was already
asleep, and lay down at my side. Sensing him there, I woke
up, but that he should not know it, I lay very still, thinking
to myself, "The man's hunger for sons amounts to the sin
of greed! Were he as greedy after food, he would by now
be too fat to move." I was weary and my heart was cold
toward him, for I knew too well that he came to get me
with child, and neither to give nor to get pleasure from me.
I was sickened when I thought of the years I had submitted
to him, bearing him son after son, ever in the hope that the
miracle would happen and his heart would warm toward
me. I had been too humble in my hopes, like a dog that
cringes back to the foot that has kicked it.

Jacob laid his hand on me, to awaken me to my duty, but I flinched at his touch.

"Leah—you are awake," he said.

I did not move or reply. He pulled me toward him, but I pulled away. It was the first time I had ever done so and he was astonished.

"Leah, don't deny me one last son. This is not like you."

"It is like me. It is what you have made me. And I will and I do deny you! Go, get you to your loved wife and leave me in peace."

"But I love you too," he said, his voice stumbling like a boy's.

"You lie," I said coldly. "You have never loved me. I have borne you all the sons I am going to bear. Begone and let me sleep, for I have earned it."

He was silent for so long I wondered if he was still there. I could not sleep as long as he was. Stealthily I reached my hand backwards to feel if the place behind me was empty. His hand caught mine and held it.

"Leah," he said, in a voice that was new to me, a voice both humble and remorseful, "forgive me if I have neglected you. It was not my fault if God put more love into my heart for Rachel. You have been all that any man could desire in a wife. And I have loved you, with what was left of myself—"

I turned over and sat up. "Do I lick out her dirty bowls? Do I pick up the skins of fruit she discards, and eat them? Nor will I be content any longer with the scraps of your love! I was trained to duty and obedience and, thanks to that, you have eleven sons today instead of five. I want no whining pleas now, for the love I had for you is dead. *You* may be able to make children lovelessly, but *I* cannot. Now get you from here, for I am finished!"

I could not see his face, but I was pleased to imagine it was shamed and humiliated. I expected him to get up and slink away, and not return. But to my shock and amazement, he flung himself upon me, bearing me down.

"You shall not reject me!" he muttered. "You are mine—you alone can still bear—God wills it! You must submit!"

But I was in no mood to submit. Middle-aged and weary I might be, but I was still strong, and Jacob had never pitted his strength against any, even as a young man. A ravisher—he? I could almost have laughed at the very notion. I pushed my forearm against his throat and threw him off without difficulty.

"God wills it—blasphemer!" I whispered, panting (only a little). "Pray for forgiveness—no, not from me," I added, as I saw from his posture that he was taking me at my word and that real shame had now overtaken him. "From God, who gave you a man's body to bring joy and rapture to a woman's and not to force her in humiliation and pain. Be ashamed, Jacob!"

"I am," he whispered. He was weeping. Now he seemed to me in the darkness almost as one of my own children, crying for his wrongdoings, needing my forgiveness. I knelt beside him and embraced him lightly. "There now, it is all over. Men are men. I should have known they cannot stand to be balked, any more than a child can."

But still he wept, his head on my shoulder. "My Leah . . . You are so kind. . . . And you did love me, I know it. Why was I so blind as not to realize the worth of what I ignored? If I could live it all again from the beginning, you should have the reverence of a queen."

I laughed a little. "The reverence of a queen! You would make but a new folly toward me then. Love of a husband for his wife—that is all I ever wanted. That is the treasure beyond treasures that I was cheated of." Suddenly, I, too, began to weep, not so much for the loss of my youth and for the loveless years, but for the loss of my love for him, which had been replaced by a kind of tender, impatient pity at best.

"Oh, Leah, Leah! I am sorry! I beg you, let me love you now, let me comfort you, for I can't bear to see you weep!"

In my weakness I let him draw me toward him; I felt his kisses—he had so seldom kissed me—falling on me softly, his lips taking up my tears. . . . I let myself be carried by my sadness into a strange dark world of gentle, fleshly tenderness that had never been between us in all the years. It was the last time. The last, and the best.

From this coupling, so different from all the others, was born to me my daughter, my only daughter, Dinah. She was the last of my children, and the dearest of all in my heart.

Four

---◄►---

Dinah

With Dinah still a baby in my arms, we set off for Beer-Sheba, in the far south, early one morning twenty years after Jacob first came to Padan-Aram.

We were a strange party. Four women, mounted on donkeys; a cluster of boys, some riding before or behind their mothers, others running beside us with long sticks to help keep the flocks together. Zilpah carried Zebulun; Rachel, Joseph; and Bilhah held my son Issachar before her on her donkey, he being nearly four years old. And with us came the men and maids of Jacob's household, for he was now a rich man.

The flocks were unusual. Every goat was striped or speckled—there was not one plain-coated among them. And the sheep were all black. There was a reason for this. When Jacob had at last requested his wages from my father, in the form of flocks, they agreed, after much haggling, that Jacob could keep all the pied or dark animals, including those that would be born in the coming spring. Our husband, clever in the ways of nature, selected from among the rams and he-goats some that were parti-colored, and brought these to the ewes and she-goats for two seasons, keeping the plain-colored males apart, until he had bred into the flock sufficient striped and spotted beasts to make up more than half the herd. We could not help laughing at my father's face as lamb after lamb, kid after kid emerged from its birth sac either wholly black or showing streaks and spots, stripes and patches, until the pen looked like a great pan of milk into which soot has been stirred. My father was fairly tearing his beard by the end; he had made the agreement because parti-colored stock is rare among our animals, and now it seemed the very gods had turned against him, for there had never been so many; and he saw that he had been tricked as he had once tricked the tricker.

Thus Jacob grew quite rich, and could have servants of his own. He even bought handmaids to serve Bilhah and Zilpah. He had camels and asses as well. I was not surprised when my brothers began to grumble, for much more than half the flock now belonged to Jacob.

"He's taken a great deal of what was yours, by cunning," one of them complained to my father. "For years you've let him take charge of the flocks because you were too lazy to oversee him yourself. We've watched him. We've seen him gaining in skill. We warned you he was dangerous to us, but you were too well satisfied to get rid of him in time. Now look! Our inheritance is dispersed. Soon he will leave with our sisters and their children and half our wealth will go with him."

But I heard my father mutter, "The man has been with me so many years, he has no will to part from me. Besides, his brother still threatens him. . . . He will never dare to go."

However, my father hadn't the wit to keep his displeasure to himself. Before long it was obvious to Jacob that Laban and his sons were sullen and angry. Perhaps it seemed safer to Jacob to brave the unknown than to stay here where he now felt threatened. So one day he brought us together and told us that God had now given him a sign that it was time to leave. We were to make our preparations quietly, saying nothing to our father or brothers, who were themselves getting ready to go out sheepshearing some distance from the town. This was usually a three- or four-day expedition, so we knew we should have a good start before they came home and discovered we had gone.

Thus it was that we set out at dawn, as I have related. After so many years of trying to persuade Jacob to leave, now that the move had come I was not happy about it, chiefly because of the tender age of some of the children, especially my little Dinah, who was the most beautiful of all my offspring but also the only one who was delicate. I carried her, with a bundle across the donkey's withers to rest my arms on. She lay there, her face protected from the glare by a veil; I could not see her clearly, but sometimes I would feel her little features with my fingers through the veil to reassure myself of her beauty, and as often as she whimpered I would open the slit in my robe and, raising the veil from the lower part of her face, put her to the breast. The rocking motion of the donkey soon put her to sleep.

To the boys, the journey was, to begin with anyway, pure delight. Despite my warnings that they would tire themselves, they ran from one end of the caravan to the other, dodging under the slow, steady legs of the camels or swinging on their necks, teasing the asses and sheep, nagging the servants for morsels of food, cautious only not to annoy their father.

We crossed a great river on the second day, at a shallow ford which Jacob led us to. The younger boys were put on the camels, but Reuben, Simeon, Levi, and Judah splashed through it, thigh-deep, laughing and throwing water at each other and pretending to swim. The men drove the flocks through, and Jacob waded back and forth, escorting the asses that carried us and the younger children. Water swirled past my knees as my unwilling beast was dragged through the ford; but Dinah lay dry on the bundle and laughed at the gurgling sound of the river.

"How is our daughter?" Jacob asked fondly.

"Well, my lord. If you contrive not to drown her, she will live to do you honor."

Ah, if I had only known! I think I would have let the river carry her little body away then.

For ten days we traveled. I had stopped turning my head every hour to see if we were being pursued, and was beginning to think more of what would happen when we encountered Esau. Surely, I thought, surely anger does not outlast twenty years! But I would have done better to keep my eyes behind me after all, for suddenly on the eleventh day the lookout at the tail of our train shouted, "Look behind! We are pursued!"

We had left the plain by this time and were climbing among the hills which are called Gilead. We could neither hide nor flee forward, and our trail was clearly marked. So we stopped, pitched camp, and waited.

Our father and brothers came up with us at evening. They had pitched their tents a short distance away, and came toward us on foot, the three of them, but with armed menservants following.

My father stopped within a few paces of us, and he and Jacob looked at each other in silence.

We women huddled together with our children in our midst, and the few men we had with us stood between us and Jacob. The boys peered between us, anxious to miss nothing, and we ourselves strained our ears to hear what was to be said.

At last my father spoke.

"What have you done?" he asked bitterly. "Why have you crept away like a thief, carrying off my daughters and grandchildren and half my wealth? Am I a tyrant, that I would not have let you go if you had come to me like a man and asked me? I would have sent you off with feasting and celebrations, I would have given you gifts—"

"Ha! Most likely," I heard Rachel mutter.

"As it is," he went on, "I could not even kiss my chil-

dren and give them my blessing. They were stolen from
me, stolen, son-in-law! What have you to say?"

Nothing, seemingly. Jacob stood mute. My father
went on.

"I have pursued you, as you see, and I have both the
right and the power to do you harm, and to take back my
daughters by force as you took them from me by stealth."

My brothers drew closer, as if waiting for a word of
command. Rachel stiffened herself beside me, and Zilpah
moaned and clutched her son; but I was not afraid.

"Bluster and ranting," I whispered. "Don't fear. He
has no right, and he knows it—this is just his way. Wait."

"But," went on my father, in a less angry and more
whining tone, "I shall restrain myself, due to a dream I had
last night, in which your God spoke to me. He told me to
leave you untouched. Therefore I may, with honor, refrain
from punishing you."

My sister relaxed with a sigh. Jacob never moved or
spoke.

"However, there is one thing which I must insist on,"
my father said. "My daughters I give to you, and all these
flocks which should have been my sons' but for your trick-
ery. . . . Nay, I withdraw that. But must you also steal
my gods? The gods of my household are gone, and it is
sure you have taken them."

To my surprise I felt Rachel stiffen again, and when
Jacob said, "I have nothing about me which belongs to
you. Search, if you do not believe me," Rachel suddenly
picked up her skirts and ran back toward the tents.

There was a movement among the people on both
sides, and a path was made for my father, who strode,
without looking at us, into our camp and began searching
for the idols. Muttering to himself, he shuffled through all
our things, feeling into the pockets of saddles, rummaging
through the piles of blankets and skins, and even picking
up rocks to see if his treasures were hidden beneath them.

"Beware that your careful search does not earn you a scorpion's sting," said Jacob, and I could tell from his voice that he was very angry.

But my father only threw him a look and went on searching. However, he found nothing, and was obliged to return to the open space between the two camps empty-handed.

When he faced my husband again, I saw murder in Jacob's face for the second time in my life. "Lay before us all you have found that is yours," he said in a low voice.

My father shrugged.

"You have lost no gods!" Jacob said furiously. "You used that only as an excuse to make a general search. Well, you have found nothing, and for nothing you have questioned my honor and accused me of thievery. In all these twenty years, what have I done to deserve this? Had your flocks been my own, I could not have given them greater care. I have not only dealt honestly with you, taking not a single lamb for myself, but I have borne the loss of even those that died through no fault of mine, and did not trouble you with tales of wild beasts, or floods, or droughts. While you slept warm in your tent, I was out in the cold night, or under the burning sun, suffering hardships of all kinds only to protect what was yours. Fourteen years I served you for Rachel and Leah, and six more for a flock of my own, and even so I feared that if I warned you of my purpose to leave, you would have found a way to send me to my own place with empty hands. Now you turn upon me like a viper and accuse me of dishonesty! Truly it is fortunate for you that I am not a violent man!"

My father backed away from him, and even my brothers stood motionless, amazed at his hard, strong speech, so unlike him. For myself, I felt proud of him and ashamed of my father, for every word was true.

No longer bold, my father spoke whiningly, as always when he was met with firmness.

"The gods are indeed missing," he said. "And my tent is empty of women and children; my sheeppens are thinly filled, and my sons abuse me. . . . No matter. We will say no more. Come, let us bring all to a good end. Promise me that you will use my daughters well, and take no more wives. Then I am satisfied."

Jacob stared at him for a moment, and then, bending down, he picked up a long stone and set it on end like a pillar.

"This is a boundary between us," he said. "This side is mine, and that side is yours. See that you never pass it to come at me, and I will leave you in peace also. As to your daughters, you need no promises from me. I will use them as I always have, no better, no worse. Now take your leave of them, for I have had my fill of you."

So our father kissed us across the pillar, and we let the boys run across to bid him good-by; I embraced my brothers, and for them I wept, but for my father—who had loved and protected me when I was young—I had no tears, for I saw him now for what he was.

Only Rachel did not come. My father said, "I bid her good-by in her tent. She is unwell."

After it was all over and my father and his party had broken camp and gone back toward Aram, I hurried to Rachel's tent. I found her seated on the ground staring ahead of her.

"What's the matter, why did you not come?" I asked. "You were well enough before."

Rachel smiled slowly.

"I am too comfortable," she said, "seated here on the saddles."

In a flash it came to me. "You! You stole the idols!"

"Yes."

"And sat on them while our father searched!"

"Yes."

"Telling him you were unwell and could not rise."

"Yes."

"But why? What do you want with them? What can such false gods matter to you now?"

After a moment, she answered, "I wished to save our father from ending his life in idolatry."

I was speechless for a moment. Then I said, "Rachel, that's a lie. You care nothing for our father or for his soul. Tell me the truth."

Rachel stood up stiffly, bent down behind her, and took the little figures out of the packs. She unwrapped them and put one in my hand.

"Feel it," she said. "Feel its weight. It is solid—it is real. One can touch and see it. One can set it up in a niche in a wall, and look at it, and make it offerings. Oh, Leah, don't look so horrified! I shall not do it, or if I do, now and then, it will not be because I worship these old gods, but because it is hard—it is very hard for me, Leah, to love a God I cannot see. I am not like you. My soul is tied to the earth and the things of the earth. I need something visible to fix my prayers upon. I shall explain to our husband's God that this little statue stands for Him. Surely He will not be angry that I have brought a little piece of my roots into the strange new life we enter. In truth, I couldn't bear to leave them."

"God may understand," I said. "But will Jacob?"

She thought for a moment. "You are right," she said. "I won't tell him." And she took the figure back from me, rolled it in its cloth again, and hid it as before.

We journeyed on, and now our thoughts were all ahead.

Jacob came to my tent one night as he often did—to play with Dinah, so he said, but really it was as much to seek my advice.

"We approach the land of Seir, which men call the Red Field," he said. "They call it that in honor of my brother Esau, whose skin and hair are that color. My blood tells me each day that I am drawing near to him. I fear him, Leah. I fear him! He has reason to hate me, even after so long. How shall I approach him? For I don't want there to be enmity between us."

I thought about the matter overnight, and the next day I suggested that Jacob send messengers ahead to Esau, taking brotherly and humble greetings, and at the same time letting him know that Jacob was now rich. "Do not send gifts yet," I said, "for if he is still your enemy he will take all that you send and may still fall upon you as you come near him. But if he is a man hungry for wealth—a kind with which I am well acquainted—such a hint may water down his rage with the hope of riches."

Jacob did as I suggested, and three days later, at evening, the messengers were back. I had word of their coming from afar, and ran to tell my husband. I have seldom seen him so agitated as he was while waiting for them, and as they toiled toward us he shouted to them to hurry.

"I hunger and thirst for the word they bring," he muttered.

The messengers stood before him at last, travel-marked and weary.

"We came to your brother," said one. "We gave him your message. He sent us back, and told us to tell you that he is coming to meet you."

"Alone?"

"No. We looked back on the way. He comes with a great company of men—perhaps four hundred or more."

Jacob threw back his head and looked up to heaven. His eyes flashed fear. "O God, guide and protect me!" I heard him whisper. Then he clenched his hands and the sweat started on his brow as he asked, "Are they far behind you?"

"Perhaps half a day's journey."

Jacob turned sharply to me. "Come, you must help me, Leah," he said, rubbing the sweat from his face. "We

must divide the camp into two. You shall be in one and
Rachel in the other, each with your own children. I will
divide the men and the flocks also. Then if Esau strikes one
camp, the other may yet escape."

"So we shall," I said. "But, husband, now is the time
to take other measures. Take from your riches all you can
spare, and more. Send drovers with goats, sheep, camels,
and oxen, and see that many young may be included, for
this always makes a flock look bigger. Send them off in
droves, one before the other, with spaces between, so that
as each meets Esau his anger may melt, little by little, as he
takes the flocks one by one to himself. Let each drover,
when Esau questions him, say that these flocks and herds
are gifts from you, and let him add that you yourself are
coming after. In that way, by the time you reach him, his
rage may be appeased."

Jacob stared at me. "You are full of wisdom," he said.

In the night, as I slept uneasily with Dinah in the crook of
my arm, Jacob came and woke me.

"I cannot rest," he said. "Let us go forward now. I
cannot wait till morning. I want to face him and have
done."

So I got ready, and soon we set off through the darkness, Jacob, Rachel and I, Zilpah and Bilhah and our sons. I
wanted to leave Dinah behind in safety, but Jacob insisted
they should all come. It was as if his guilt and fear had
pushed him to a point where he felt only by risking all his
family could he appease Esau. At the last minute, however,
my terrors for her were too great. I hid her in a chest,
propping open the lid, and rolled up a bundle of cloth to
carry instead. Let Jacob throw us all to the red lion, but
my darling should be safe!

We traveled to a river, where there was a shallow
ford, and again Jacob helped us over. It was still black-

dark and the crossing would have unnerved me if I had had
Dinah in my arms; as it was I was too busy worrying
whether the maid I had bribed would remember to feed
her. In the darkness all was noise and splashing and confusion, and then at last we were all on the other side and everything became quiet. We stood close together on our
donkeys, with the little boys huddled close to us.

"Where is Jacob?" I asked into the darkness.

No one knew.

"He led my ass across," said Rachel. "Then he left me
here and turned back across the river." Zilpah and Bilhah
said the same, and the boys said he had carried them over,
one or two at a time. But now he was not among us.

We strained our eyes. I of course could see nothing at
all, but Rachel said, "The moon will rise soon; then we will
know where he is." And after a short time, she let out a little cry.

"The moon has risen! And see—there he is—!"

"Where?" asked the others.

"There, do you not see him? Back on the far bank.
But who is that with him? Leah, can you see?"

"Nothing! What is it?"

"It is a man, a tall man! I'm sure he is not one of our
people from the camp—we have none built like him."

"Aiii! They are struggling together!" cried Zilpah.

"Rachel! Who is it?" I asked, clutching her arm in
terror. "Is it Esau?"

"I don't know, I don't know! Jacob!" she called
affrightedly across the rustling water. But there was no
reply.

"See? They're wrestling!" exclaimed Reuben excitedly. "They have no weapons. They are locked together,
Mother, swaying to and fro! He is bigger than Father, yet
Father holds him squarely and does not give ground. How
can it be? Our father has never used his strength in his
life!"

"Once he did," breathed Rachel. "Once—when he lifted the stone from the mouth of the well. That day he had the strength of three."

"See how they pant and strain!" cried Levi, jumping about. "Hold him, Father, push him down! Get your foot behind him! Oh, why does it have to be night? I can't see properly!"

"Father must lose," said Simeon. "I will go back across the river and help him. Such a contest is unfair, the man is twice his size!"

But I clenched both hands on his garments to restrain him.

"You will not go," I said. "Your father would call you if he needed help. Let him do his own fighting. Tell me what is happening!"

So we all stood on the far bank and gradually the excitement died down, for in truth nothing much did happen so far as could be seen—Jacob and the other man stood chest to chest, struggling and panting, their feet planted apart, their knees and thighs pressed together. Occasionally we would hear a grunt or a gasp, and sometimes one of my sons would shout, "See, he has changed his hold, now Father must give way! See, he sways, he will be down!" Yet always, somehow, Jacob recovered and did not fall.

The strangest of all the strange things was that it went on and on. The moon climbed the sky, then sank again and at last set; the boys, worn out, first sat down to watch and then slipped into sleep against the legs of the beasts; gradually even we women found our heads nodding. And still the two figures stood there, locked and unyielding.

I slept where I sat, on the ass's back.

A sudden movement startled me awake. The ass was moving. I opened my eyes. The sun was up. A dark shape was in front of me, pulling the ass along. "Who is it, who is it?" I asked in panic.

"It's your husband, who else?" answered a weary voice.

"Jacob! Is it really you?" I reached out to touch him, to reassure myself. Had the whole thing been a dream?

"It is me," he said.

The other women, and the boys, were hurrying to catch us up. Rachel was still sleeping on her donkey, which Jacob led with his other hand.

"Jacob! What happened? Who was it? Where is he?"

"Be silent. I am tired to death."

When the others drew level with us, I motioned them sternly to be quiet and not to disturb Jacob, who dragged his feet and limped as he walked, and often seemed rather to hold himself up by the asses' heads than pull them along. But after a while, as the sun became higher and hotter, he seemed to recover somewhat, and when we stopped to eat, I ventured to ask as I served him, "Who was that stranger beyond the river? We feared for you."

"I don't know," he said, and then added strangely, "he was the one I saw before, on the ladder. But he would not tell me his name."

"Why did he struggle against you?"

"It was a trial."

"And who triumphed?"

He ate a little in silence, and then said slowly, "He could have broken me between finger and thumb. Yet he said, 'You have striven with God and with men, and you have prevailed.' In truth, Leah, our God is hard to understand."

"Did he say more?"

"He said I am not to be called Jacob any longer, but Israel."

"What does such a name mean?"—for with us every name has a meaning, and this was a strange name to me.

"It means, 'He who strives with God,'" said my husband with a look of awe.

Cold waves passed over my body.

"Are you saying that that stranger whom we saw, was —God?"

"Nay, do not ask me. I don't know."

"And you took no hurt?"

"As the sun rose he touched my thigh, only touched it —and now I am lame in that leg as you saw."

One more question came to my mouth. I wanted to know why he had gone back across the river after seeing us safely across. The only answer I could think of was so discreditable to my husband—I so little wanted to hear, or even suspect, that he had been seized by fear and had been prevented only by the stranger from fleeing and abandoning us all there—that I shut my lips.

"You are tired, my lord," I said instead. "Let's rest here a little before going on."

But before he could reply, there was a cry from one of the boys, who was scouting on the edge of our group.

"Father, Father! He's coming. Look—a great dust cloud!"

Jacob grew white and got up hurriedly. The light was brilliant by now. He shaded his eyes and peered south—we all did, even I, who could see nothing but a bright, dusty blur.

"It is Esau," said Jacob in a toneless voice. "The time is come."

But instead of gathering us at once about him and preparing to march to meet his brother—and his fate, for I knew well that it was for this that he had made us all accompany him—my husband fell to the ground and lay there on his face. We women stood a little apart, with the children, watching him; we did not know what to do, for without him to guide us we were lost, and Rachel began to tremble and Bilhah to weep.

Zilpah, however, was of stronger stuff. She came to me and whispered, "What is with my lord? Is he praying, or has he fainted from weakness after the struggles of the night?"

I shook my head. We waited a little longer. Jacob looked lifeless. Judah, my eight-year-old, ran to me.

"Mother, Mother! Make Father get up! Our uncle is coming—I can see him now, he is red and fearsome with a great beard like a flame and he is as tall as a giant!"

But it was Joseph who roused Jacob in the end. Joseph was, apart from Dinah, his favorite child; and when he ran to him and threw himself on the ground at his side, crying and whimpering in fear, Jacob seemed to come to himself. He rose slowly and stiffly, wiping the sand and sweat from his face, and comforted the little boy, saying, "Nay, son, don't cry. See, your father, who has most to fear, stands on his legs and does not tremble. Go to your mother now, and be a man, and stand to her defense."

Then came a moment which would stand out as one of the bitterest in my life, had there not been others more bitter still. For in his fear for himself and us, Jacob now showed again, too plainly, where his heart still clung. For he arranged us thus: first our handmaids, who were his concubines, with their children behind them; then I and mine; and last of all, hidden behind me where they might not be seen and might escape Esau's wrath, he placed Rachel and Joseph.

He came to me. "Give Dinah to me," he said.

"What do you want with her?"

"I will give her to Rachel to hold, that she may be in less danger than if she is here in the second rank with you."

I turned my almost-blind eyes upon him.

"You show your preference without shame, my lord," I said. "But Dinah's life is safer than you guess. She is in the last rank of all, being the most precious of all—she is back in the camp, where I left her. Here." I held out to him the false bundle I had been carrying. "Take this token of her, with which I have deceived you, and with it in your arms, march to meet your brother. Perhaps he may hesitate to kill you with a baby in your arms."

Now he could feel the trembling of the ground as the men of Esau—fully four hundred, as I afterward learned, sons, armed servants, and men of Seir—tramped toward us. I could hear the low thunder of their feet and their voices. Jacob let the bundle fall and turned from me to face them.

I called my son Reuben to me.

"Be my eyes," I said as soon as he stood beside me.

His tale was broken up by his childishness, for at times he became too engrossed in the scene before him to remember to report it to me. I could feel him moving under my hand, craning his neck and jumping to make sure he missed nothing.

"The big red man, our uncle, has stopped. He is still quite far from us . . . his men are behind him—very many, Mother, and they have weapons, and they look fiercely on us. . . . The dust is blowing toward us, they seem as if in a brown mist, but the big man's beard still appears like a beacon through it. . . . Do you think he means us harm?"

"Your father—tell me about him."

"Father is walking slowly, slowly toward them. Oh! Now he has fallen down again—no—he is all right—he was bowing to my uncle—now he is up again and walking nearer—the dust has come around him—Down again! His face is on the ground, his hands before him—he has risen—Why does he keep bowing down, Mother? Is his brother so much greater than he that Father must bow to him again and again as he gets nearer? Oh, look!" He stopped.

I squeezed his shoulder hard in my impatience.

"I cannot look, boy. Tell me what you see!"

"Something so strange, Mother! My uncle was carrying his spear as if ready for a fight, but now he is lowering it. Father is almost up to him now. Surely he sees Father is unarmed, and that he has only us with him? Yes—see—he has dropped the spear altogether, and with one hand he is signaling his men to fall back. Now the two of them stand together alone in the cloud of dust." Again a silence from my witness.

"Well? Well? What now?"

"Nothing. That is the strange thing. They stand facing each other, two paces apart."

"Are they speaking?"

"It's hard to see—I don't think so—no part of them moves at all—oh—oh!"

"Reuben, would you drive me mad? Speak, what is happening?"

"Why, Mother," said my son in a tone of wonder, "they have come together. They embrace. They are kissing!"

My legs gave under me. I sank to the ground and wept with relief. Reuben hardly noticed. It was Zilpah who crouched to help me up. She was crying too—Zilpah who was so calm and strong.

"Why do you weep?" I whispered to her. "Were you also afraid?"

"I was afraid," she admitted, "but I think it is not for that. It is a pity you did not see it, mistress. When they fell on each other's necks—why, it was—I can't say how it was. But I shall not forget how my heart twisted in me, not till my dying hour."

The tension was broken. The boys broke ranks and leaped and rolled in the sand, laughing and pummeling each other in their joy and relief. Two of mine—Levi and Simeon—even dared to make little dashes in the direction of their huge uncle, their courage always failing before they got to him, so that they came racing back, half terrified by their own daring.

I caught Simeon as he fled past me.

"What are they doing now?"

"They're talking, Mother. Uncle Esau is so big! He has red hair like me. Will I have a beard like that? Will he let me touch it? Oh, I'm glad he's not going to kill us!"

Reuben was more thoughtful. "Why did Father let us think our uncle was so bad, Mother? He's not bad. See, he's smiling, and he has his arm around Father. Father's weeping—"

"Reuben, leave them alone. Run and play now."

"No, I can't. Look, Father's beckoning us all to come. Come on, Mother, don't fear! We'll protect you."

We all drew near to the two brothers, who stood together talking. As I approached I heard Jacob say, "Yes, these are the children God has graciously given to your servant." And the big man turned and put out his hands and touched each boy as Jacob said his name in order of their age. We four women bowed down and Esau greeted us all in a deep, thick voice, but kindly. Then he said to Jacob, "What was the meaning of all the flocks and herds that I met on the way?"

"Did the shepherds not give you my message?" asked Jacob, in such an astonished tone that I realized at once that he thought Esau had been appeased only by the gifts. "Why," he went on in even greater puzzlement, "I see now the flocks I sent before me are not with you. Did you not understand they were my gifts to you?"

There was silence, and then Esau said slowly, "I have enough. Listen, brother. Keep what is yours; I don't want it."

I needed no eyes to know that such an answer was the last that Jacob was prepared for, and that it confounded him.

And now he began to plead, in a tone I had never heard him use—a tone, in fact, that reminded me uncomfortably more of my father Laban than of my husband.

"Nay, I pray you, if you would please me, accept the gifts from my hands. To see your face again, and to see it clean of all anger and enmity against me, is as good to my eyes as to see the face of God Himself. So take my offerings, for otherwise I shall not believe that I have found favor in your sight and that we are brothers again."

Esau was so long answering that I thought he had moved away; but venturing to raise my eyes, I saw his tall figure standing there. At last he said in a muffled voice, "If you urge me on your own account, then let it be as you wish."

"You'll take them?" asked Jacob, almost shrill with relief.

"Yes."

"I thank you, brother! I thank you for your goodness!" And Jacob embraced him again.

Later he was to say, "He only needed urging. I knew all the time he must take them in the end. How else could I have faced him, had he proved to be a man satisfied with his lot, who would accept no riches from one who had wronged him? Such men do not exist in common life. He has changed much with the years, but no man changes out of recognition." Indeed, I do not know how he would have borne himself if Esau had not taken the gifts. And it was never known to me in what spirit he had taken them— whether to gratify his own ambition as Jacob supposed, or to do his brother good. But I had my own ideas about it.

I never got to know my brother-in-law, for almost at once he turned with his men and returned to Seir, after arranging with Jacob to follow in his own time because of the tender age of the children. But I was not too surprised when, as we journeyed on (now rejoined by all our people whom we'd left on the other side of the river, and I with Dinah once more in my arms) we traveled west instead of following Esau to the south. It seemed that my husband, even after the evidence Esau had given him of his willingness to forgive, was still happiest when far from his company. And I have not seen him from that day to this . . . which, to my mind, is a pity.

Our next place of settlement was one that I prefer not to remember now.

It was outside the city of Salem. It was a poor sort of place to call itself a city. Its houses were generally low and mean, its people—five or six large families in all—ill-dressed, its men ungentle and surly. When we pitched our tents outside its walls, not intending to remain long, the inhabitants of the town drifted out to look us over, and were impressed by what they saw—so impressed that Jacob was fearful lest, in their own low condition, they try to steal what was ours. But we were well supplied with men to guard us, and after one or two meetings with the chief lord of the place (who called himself Hamor and a "prince" of the Hivite tribe, though he had nothing princely in his looks to my eyes), it was reasonably clear that they wanted no trouble with us.

So we stayed there, and the children grew. The boys grew like wild vines, untrained, untrammeled; there were too many of them for any one father to control, and I—I fear I was too easy with them, for I was getting old and fat; *I* could not chase them and chastise them once they were big enough to dash from my side at first light and not return until their stomachs forced them home. They were like a tribe of young wolves, wandering the area, picking and despoiling where they would. Only Reuben and Joseph proved tractable. Reuben, as the eldest, was kept at his father's side to learn those things an heir must learn; and besides, he was not a wild one like his brothers, but rather quiet and dignified like Jacob (though, like him, unstable).

And Joseph? Joseph, I have to own it, was the best of

them all. Jacob loved him and said he was closest akin to
his father, Isaac. He alone would come to our tent and sit
with us women in the evenings, or help us to lift the heavy
jars of oil, water, wine, and corn, and tell us tales to pass
the time as we grew older. He would tell us his dreams,
which were often most strange. He made no distinction between us; we were all four his mothers, and indeed, twenty
such would not have been too many for him to love and be
loved by.

My lot at this time was not unhappy, though God
knows I realize now I should have been deeply concerned
about the characters of my sons. But my one daughter was
such a joy to me that, in truth, I thought little about them.
As she grew, I knew by touching her that she was growing
more and more beautiful—like Rachel, only with reddish
hair, and more strength in her features. *She* did not distrib-
ute her love equally among all the wives of her father. For
her, one mother was enough, and that was I. To the rest
she was mannerly in all things, and helpful, and tender as
they grew older; but for me she kept her special love, and I
basked in it, as old bones always bask in sunlight.

But she, too, had an unbiddable streak in her.

As the years passed, it was natural that she, as the only
maiden in our family, deprived of sisters or companions of
her own level of life, should seek for friends among the
girls of the town. They had a meeting place ready made:
the well outside the city walls. There is a tradition in our
family that wells are places of destiny for our womenfolk.
At a well was Jacob's mother chosen for his father. At a
well Rachel first met Jacob. And now it was at the well of
Salem that Dinah was to meet her fate (may God shut His
ears as I tell it, lest even His heart break at it!).

Thus, when Dinah would go with her jar to bring our
water, she would meet her friends from the families within
the city walls, and talk to them. Often she would chatter to
me of this one or that one, and many times I urged her to

bring them back to our tent. But she never did, and I understood it was because she was ashamed of our way of life, for still Jacob did not build us a house, saying we were not yet done with our wanderings.

I did not wish Dinah to go into the city. It had seemed to me, the rare times I had been there (I never went alone) to have about it an air of poverty, ignorance, and evil. Their gods were all heathen idols, and their ways were not our ways. Though I could not stop Dinah from having friends among them, I feared for her should she go alone among their homes and streets and menfolk. And our sons were forbidden to make acquaintance with the daughters of the city.

These restrictions placed a strain upon our sons, who were now full-grown, even Joseph being fourteen, and often we urged Jacob to move on; but yet again he had sunk into a lethargy and would not heed us. I must say that the worst we thought of was that one of the lads would bring home a Hivite girl as a wife, something we did not wish for, since we despised those people for their idolatrous and base ways; my care of Dinah was no more than the ordinary watch any mother keeps over a beautiful young daughter.

Then one day, a day of most cursed memory, she was late home from the well.

Lazy, old, careless as I was, I did not at first notice how late it was. But when Zilpah came to me and said, "Where is Dinah with the water? It is time to prepare the evening meal," then my heart beat sharp and sudden and I asked, "Is it dark outside?" When she said, "Yes, this hour or more," I felt fear of a most unusual sort stirring in me as it had not stirred since I stood with Reuben facing the oncoming of Esau.

Seeing my hand on my breast and hearing me whimper, Zilpah said hurriedly, "Do not say she has not returned! Oh, God protect her! Nay, but don't trouble

yourself yet, mistress. I will send Gad to find her." But to
find Gad was the first task, for it was not yet suppertime
and he might yet be an hour's travel from the camp. However, after half that time she found him, and his brother
Asher with him, and together she sent them off in haste
and with hot words of urging behind them to the city gates
to seek their half sister.

They returned empty-handed, having found no trace
of her.

Now the camp was fully aroused. Jacob, on hearing
Dinah was missing, flew into one of his rare passions, berating himself, and me, for failing to take better charge of his
treasure, and her brothers (especially my sons, who were
her full brothers) for not guarding her as was their duty.
He lashed them all with his tongue until their very souls
must have been blistered, and then, choosing three of them
—Reuben as the eldest, Simeon, the tallest and fiercest-
looking, and Judah, who had the greatest gift with words,
he sent them into Salem with orders to go to the house of
the "prince," and to say there that if their sister was not
found and returned with all speed, and safely, into their
hands, they and their kinsmen and servants would lay
waste to the city before morning.

More, I fear, through seeing in this a welcome cause
for a real quarrel than out of devotion to their sister, the
brothers one and all (saving only Joseph, who was still out
with the sheep) insisted upon going together. And so they
set off, ten of them, well-armed, and we hoped to see them
bearing Dinah back to us (though in what case I dared not
think) within the hour. I spent the time praying, weeping,
and wringing my hands. For each moment that passed was
a moment that could be bringing about my daughter's ruin.

They tramped back with faces blacker than the darkness now all around us, and stood in a half circle around
our campfire.

"Well? Well?" cried Jacob. "What did Hamor say?"

Hamor was the old prince's name. "Why do you not bring her? Would he not send men to seek her out?"

"He had no need," growled Levi. "He knows well where she is. She is with his own son, Shekhem."

Even as I threw myself, wailing and tearing my clothes, upon the ground, Jacob rose up.

"What!" he roared. "And you left her there?"

"We had no choice," said Reuben. "All his people were about him when he spoke to us. Besides—"

"Speak!" shouted their father, in a tone I had never heard.

"Hamor said he would come himself, tomorrow, to speak with you."

"To speak with me!" cried Jacob from his very bowels. "He comes to speak with me! He comes to forfeit his life if he steps out of those gates! Oh, cowards, cowards, cowards!" And he took his staff and struck among his sons, who shrank and put up their arms to shield their heads. "Sooner should you have lost your miserable lives than come back to me without her! Tomorrow, you say? You dare say to me tomorrow? Look at your mother! How shall she live through the night, until this tomorrow you speak of!"

"As well tomorrow as tonight," muttered Naphtali. "It is too late to save her honor. Must we all die for what is already lost?"

At these words I set up such a cry of mourning that must have been heard within the city walls, perhaps by the very devil Shekhem himself. I knew him—oh, I knew him! I had heard of him from Rachel, who had seen him at the well and in the market, eying the maidens and making free with those who would let him. "Handsome and rich enough to buy whom he desires," she had said. "All the wealth of the world," I had answered, "buys not our Dinah from us, to live in shame among idolators."

And now—no purchase, but theft, and a dishonor I had not dreamed of.

In vain Jacob tried to drive our sons back to the city to recapture her by force. Even when all our strength was gathered, it was not enough—and Dan said this, who was the wisest, and whose judgment we were accustomed, even at his young age, to respect.

"Naphtali is right," he said. "We do no good now by flinging ourselves one by one upon their spears. But she must be avenged. We will go about it by stealth, so that the death of Dinah's honor shall not be followed by the death of all her brothers; yet her ravisher shall not live."

"Not he, nor any of his kinsmen," added Simeon, who had kept very quiet till now. "That evil old father of his, with his smiles and his spreading hands and his honeyed speech—he shall be my special care when the time comes. Had Reuben not restrained me, his wicked head should have left his body then and there."

Levi, Judah, and Issachar murmured a fierce agreement.

Their words brought me no comfort, but more fear, more grief, for I knew what must follow and that I could not prevent it even if I would.

There was no sleep for any that night. We all sat wakeful, and the boys—men, I must call them now—clustered together around a separate fire and talked. Jacob wept silently. I had no more tears.

In the morning, Dan came to Jacob.

"Father," he said, "the villain prince is coming. No, do nothing. Vengeance is with us. Do not arouse his suspicion if you would have us live. Receive him and hear his words. Trust us, they shall be among the last he ever speaks." Rachel said she could see Hamor walking toward the camp. He had armed men with him. I went to my tent and lay there, for I could not bear to be near him. After a long time, Jacob came to me.

"He is gone."

"What did he say? What could he say?"

"You ask well," he said grimly. "If one of my sons did thus, I would have no words; yet he had many, and all smooth and gentle. He does not deny the act, nor its shame. He groveled in the dust before me, to beg pardon for his son. The boy has for long been loose-lived and immoral. His father says he has always feared some scandal of this kind. Yet now it has come, it brings a strange, unforeseen change to his son. It seems that Dinah is not despised by him as one would expect after such a deed. The opposite is true—her purity and goodness have won his heart, and he cleaves to her and craves her for his wife."

"And did you pretend to agree?"

"Leah," he said slowly. "We did well to listen to Dan. Nothing should be done in haste. The harm is done to Dinah; it is sure she will never marry any other now, for none will have her. This young man is wealthy; they own half the city, and he has offered any dowry we care to ask. His father says that although he has been wild, he has many good qualities, and that he, himself, will see that he treats her honorably. Out of a foul beginning, good may yet come."

I could not believe my ears.

"Good?" I cried. "Good out of evil? First to despoil her, then to wed her? Are we to give her to such a one as this, because now he has made her fit for nothing better? No, my lord, no, no, never! Let her return to us, let us cherish her and not revile her! She shall live safe and beloved in her mother's tent, never more to know fear or shame or pain. Do not be tempted by their riches to do her so much wrong as marry her to a ravisher because he has a smooth-tongued father!"

"But Leah—perhaps she herself would prefer—"

"She herself? She is my daughter! Thirteen years I have seen her, known and loved her, day and night, day and night! Had she had the means, she would have died before this thing happened to her. To give herself in a mockery of honorable marriage now to such a husband would be worse than death to her. Honor, Jacob! Have you forgotten *honor?*"

Jacob said nothing for a long time. Then he sighed heavily and said, "Let us discuss the matter with Dan."

He called to Dan. Reuben came with him. Jacob ordered the others to stay outside. Then he told the two of them—the eldest and the wisest—what had passed between him and Hamor and asked their advice.

"It is not only your sister who was spoken of," he said. "This prince has more in view by way of connecting us with his people. He says it is a pity that we have lived outside the walls for so long, and kept ourselves separate. He begs that this forced mingling between his son Shekhem and Dinah will lead to more general union—that the daughters of their people shall be given to my sons and that their sons shall wed the maidens of my servants. In his plan, our tribe is to join with theirs in this way, until we are all one tribe, living together in peace and prosperity."

"Prosperity—yes," said Dan. "I wondered when we should come to that. For his people are few and poor, and have neither the thrift nor the industry to raise themselves to our level of life. Even though we live in tents, our riches are as palaces compared to their wretched hovels. Nothing they put their hands to prospers, while everything we touch—thanks to your skills, Father, which you have passed to some of us—multiplies and increases our wealth."

Reuben had been staring at Dan. Now he turned eagerly to his father.

"All that may be true," he said excitedly, "but think!

If our tribes were combined, it might be to the good of us all. Some of us are sick of this wandering life. Their houses may not be much, but at least they are solid; they cleave to the ground; no cold wind blows through them on winter nights, and in summer they are cool. A man who lives in a house has a place in the world—he has dignity. This town and its surroundings are our home now—we are used to them. Asher has already begun to plant vines and grain. Others of us have seen that much could be done with the land. Can we not make this our final stopping place?"

"It can't be," said Jacob. "This is not the land that God promised to my father and grandfather."

"Then in the name of that same God, Father," said Reuben, "why do we linger here so long? If we had left earlier, as our mother so often urged, this with our sister would never have happened!"

Jacob hid his face and groaned.

"God has not given me the sign," he muttered.

Dan and Reuben exchanged looks.

"Perhaps He has now," said Dan quietly.

"But it's a pity," said Reuben. "They are not a bad people, these Hivites. I myself have seen a girl who—Not that I speak now because of her. But for all their poverty and laziness, they are a quiet, friendly tribe, and we could do well, for them and by them, if we heeded the old prince's words."

With difficulty, I drew myself to my feet.

"Have you so soon forgotten Dinah's honor?" I asked Reuben, my voice broken with grief and shame, as much for him now as for her, for here was proof that he would go which way the wind of advantage blew him, without regard for the laws and customs that had kept us an upright people for so long.

"Mother," said Reuben pleadingly, "don't look at me as if I were not your son. Don't you know what will happen if we go Simeon's and Levi's way? Believe me, I don't like to speak so of my own brothers but you know it is true, they care less for Dinah's honor than I do—much less, for I do care for it. They are straining to be off to the city and use their swords. And I tell you, if once their rage is let loose, there may be more dead afterward than the guilty only. Would you have a whole cistern of blood spilled for Dinah? *Her* gentle spirit would not want it. And how do you know what her feelings are? Many a maiden's heart turns to the man who takes her maidenhead, no matter how it comes about. See how she has made of him a man of tenderness and honor, who desires to right her and keep her with him forever! He cannot be all bad. Might she not be better off with him than spending her life in lonely barrenness?"

I had never heard Reuben speak so. For a moment I was swayed. Then I hardened my heart, for honor and custom must come first, or nothing is left.

"No," I said. "I cannot believe she would choose to live in shame with him, rather than in self-respect alone. But even if she would—for she is still young—we must prevent it. As to the killing . . . I will speak to Simeon and Levi, for there is truth in what you say of them, they may well exceed their duty; but you will go with them to restrain them. Let them punish only those who connived at the deed, and the ravisher himself, of course. While he lives, your sister is no better than a harlot."

Jacob said, "Dan. Yours is the best head. Say your say, for there is not much time."

Dan sighed and shrugged. "Nay, Father, what is there for me to say? I am not yet old enough to judge such a matter. I feel some of the anger and blood lust in the breasts of my two brothers, who sit outside even now sharpening their weapons, for I love Dinah, and she has been most cruelly wronged. I see advantages and disadvantages on all sides. Perhaps it is best that we do as Mother says—kill those who must die, and then be gone from here as from a place accursed and go to the land of your inheritance."

After a long moment, Jacob sighed in his turn and said, "But how is this righteous vengeance to be carried out? They will be expecting something. I am old, and I do not wish my sons brought back to me one by one upon litters."

Dan turned to the mouth of the tent. "This is Simeon's business," he said. "Come out and speak to him, for he has a plan that it is not good our womenfolk should hear."

When they were gone from the tent, I threw myself again upon the ground. I did not weep now but lay there in misery, plagued by doubts. I had seen much bloodshed in my life, but never by my children. Was there a blood lust in me, too, that I could give the advice I had given, that would turn at least two of my sons into killers? Yet when I thought of them, setting out to do justice and to bring Dinah back to me, I felt but a twinge compared to my overbearing agony the night before when they returned hangdog and empty-handed.

Rachel sat beside me. She had kept close to me during all that the last day and night had brought. I had been too full of anguish to notice her, but now I felt her stroking my hair and I reached out a groping hand to take hers and hold it. It came to me that there was some likeness to that other moment of closeness, long ago, when it was she who lay with rent garments and dust-filled hair, and I who sat by her and gave her comfort.

"Is this what it all comes to?" I said in a muffled voice. "Is it for this that we suffer the pangs of childbirth, to suffer more pangs, even stronger, as they grow up? Who knows if I shall ever see my sons again?" And I wailed, long and loud into the dust.

"At least you have several," said Rachel. "And most of them are fighters who will sell their lives dearly. But I—I have but one, my Joseph. . . . Is he to go too? Must he, at his tender age, go with the others and take part in the slaughter? I would give my life to keep him from even witnessing it! He is so gentle, so sensitive—Leah, it will kill him to see it! And if one attacked him, and he had, perforce, to do violence himself . . . He will never be the same again, for as much as it is in Simeon's nature to kill, it is quite out of Joseph's. Oh, is there not some way I can prevent his going? Some—some way?" And she took her hand from mine and held her head in her arms and wailed as I had, though more softly. I felt for her, and knew that I was not alone in my sorrow; so I sat up and we comforted each other.

It was then she told me her secret: that she was once again with child. She, too, had put on flesh in later years, and it was not surprising that none had noticed, for no one looked to see more children from Rachel who had been unfruitful for so many years, and besides, our loose garments hide this condition until the last. It seemed that her time was not far off, and the thought that God might be giving her this last, late child because He meant to take Joseph from her was preying on her mind.

While we spoke softly together, I felt a bright light fall on my face as the tent flap opened. Simeon and Levi came in.

"Mother," said Simeon, "we are going now to the city. But don't fear, there will be no trouble yet. We are going to speak to the old prince, to tell him our conditions for accepting his offer." If it had not been so impossibly out of keeping, I would have thought I heard laughter in his voice.

"What's this!" I cried. "You are accepting!" I was

shocked to feel some relief in my heart, and I heard Rachel give a gasp of joy at my side.

"It depends, Mother, it depends," said Levi—and here, too, I heard something like a chuckle, but there was that in it so malicious that it was scarcely kin to true laughter. I clutched both their arms.

"Sons, there is something here that turns my blood cold. What is it that makes you laugh at such a moment?"

"Don't fear, Mother!" they both said, jumping to their feet and freeing themselves. "We will soon be back." And they kissed me and hurried away.

As soon as they were gone, I called Jacob and questioned him.

"They have some plan, I know not what," he said. "They would not tell me. Leah, they are fully grown. The matter is in their hands, and seemingly they have all agreed. They told me only that by this means they could take vengeance without danger to themselves. For this we must be thankful."

"They *all* agreed?" asked Rachel quickly. "Joseph too?"

"No," said Jacob after a pause. "Joseph knows nothing of the matter. They said he was too young, and sent him off with the sheep."

"Thank you, God," whispered Rachel, and, rising, she went quietly back to her own tent. I thought to myself, "Zebulun is no older, yet he would not let himself be left behind. . . ." And I did not know whether to be proud or grieved.

Three days then passed. No three days in my life were ever longer. How could it be that matters went on as usual, while Dinah . . . ? Yet they did. We rose at dawn, prepared food, attended to all the duties of women. The men went about their concerns. The people of our tents whispered much, but were silent when they saw one of our family. And my sons whispered too. Sometimes I heard sharp bursts of that evil laughter which frightened me more than I can describe. Apart from that—and the terrible emptiness where Dinah should have been—all was as if nothing had happened.

On the third day, at evening, Simeon and Levi came to me again.

They knelt down before me and Simeon said, very solemnly this time, "Give us your blessing, Mother. For now we go to fetch Dinah."

I put my hands upon them, hands that trembled.

"You are instruments of God's justice," I said. "Remember that. Remember that every human being came out of the womb of such as your mother is, and that these products of her pain are not to be lightly sent out of this world." Suddenly my hands, acting by themselves, clasped their two heads and drew them to my breast. "My sons, my own dear sons!" I whispered. "Be men, as I made you, and not beasts. And take care of yourselves, that you return to me with your bodies as well as your honors whole and unbroken! For I love you both, and I'm afraid."

I felt a tremor pass through Levi. Simeon was tense and rigid. Then I released them and they stood up and left me.

Alas, alas for what happened next! Till this day, I ask myself: If I had known what they went to do, and what had gone before, could I have done anything to prevent it? Women are so helpless. It is wrong that they should be so, when without them there would be no men! But I did not know. I knew nothing, until I heard, drifting down to us from over the walls of the town, borne on the wind as innocently as the smoke from their fires, the first terrible screams.

I rushed from my tent. Once again, we women clung to each other, powerless to do anything but *feel*, as behind those blank walls slaughter and chaos spread. We could hear the sounds. . . . Oh, if God spares me till I am a hundred years old—and I pray daily that He will not—those cries will sound in my ears till the end: the sounds of the sons of my flesh, laying waste the life of a whole town.

Rachel was too stunned to speak, but Zilpah at last found voice to tell me that our sons were returning, driving flocks before them, and bringing with them a large crowd of women and children. In front were Simeon and Levi, each with a young girl weeping and crying; their blood-steeped swords were still out. Bilhah gave a cry.

"Smoke is rising over the walls! They have fired the town!"

"O God, forgive them! O God, forgive them!" was all Rachel could say.

But as I heard the beat of many feet approaching and smelled the dust and smoke, I screamed out, "Oh, most wicked men! Wild beasts of prey that I have raised up to fill me with shame and sorrow! What have you done, men of wrath, what have you done?"

And then Simeon stood before me, panting, and I smelled the blood, and his sweat, the sweat of a butcher. And he said to me between gasps, "What have we done, Mother? We have brought your daughter home to you. Is that not what you bid us to do?"

He stepped aside and beckoned. And Issachar, my young giant of a son, came forward. He was sobbing like a woman. And he carried Dinah, fainting, in his arms.

"Lay her at our mother's feet," said Simeon, his voice as hard as stone. "And if you blame any, Mother, blame her. For she was the cause of it all."

"Nay, give her to me!" I cried, and took her from Issachar. "How, how is she the cause, poor innocent child? It is your own cruelty that has caused this horror!"

"Mother, you don't know," said Levi. "She would not come! We had to drag her forth, and still she clung to her ravisher, and would not let him go until we slew him. Then his old father the prince, weak as he was, roused up his men, weak as *they* were, and they tried to attack us, so we had to slay them all. As for the rest—"

"The whole town was accursed!" shouted Simeon. "Every man of them was ready to see our sister dishonored in order to take a share of our flocks and cattle! Why else should all have agreed to be circumcised in order to join us? Greed, only greed deadened them to fear and pain. Headlong they rushed to do our bidding, and made no complaint! Every man in that town agreed to make our ways his ways—not because our ways are better, but because we have more, and they hungered for it, so much that their own flesh was less precious to them. It was right that we slew them all. Now it is we who can claim all that was theirs, their wives, their children, their meager flocks. They are ours now, and it is better for them to belong to us than to such feeble wretches as we put to the edge of our swords. Cease weeping, you foolish women!" he cried, turning to his captives. "Rejoice that you are fallen among men of strength who worship the true God."

"Be silent, you blasphemous whelp!"

The voice rang out into the twilight like the shrill call of the ram's horn. Every other sound ceased, except a few stifled whimperings and the heavy, exhausted breathing of the killers.

Jacob strode among them and they fell back.

"Dare not to mention the name of the Most Holy while your hands reek with the blood of those to whom you pledged your word!" he cried. No trace of his age, his uncertainty, or his weakness could be heard or seen in him now. Oh, had he always appeared before his sons as he did then, when it was too late, how might they have been different!   .

"You are mine and I did not keep you from this wickedness, therefore the shame of what you have done is mine also. But at least I do not claim righteousness, nor say that God was on my side in the deed! God gave us our freedom, to do good or evil, and you have done such evil that my heart shrivels at it. So that was your plan, to make it a condition of our union with the people of that town that the males should be circumcised as we are—and when they did this, in good faith, and had not yet recovered, then did you fall upon them in your guile and slaughter them before they were aware. Shame, shame, shame most horrible! To use God's covenant with Abraham as a means to avenge your sister's honor without risk to your worthless selves! And now you lay blame upon Dinah, for not delivering up to your swords the man who had sworn to love her. Truly, I know you not! You are no sons of mine." His voice had cracked and he was weeping even as I wept.

"But, Father," said Levi, aghast, "would you have had us pass over the deed? Should one deal with our sister as with a harlot?"

"Do not speak to me," said Jacob brokenly. "Go from this place and plunge your swords into the sand. Wash your bodies, rub coarse sand upon them, bow yourself down and humble your hearts before God. If the surrounding tribes do not come upon us and slay us all for this disgraceful treachery, it may be a sign that God can forgive you, not for your own sakes, but for love of those gentler than you who knew Him before you."

One by one they slunk away. Only Dan paused.

"*We* did none of the killing, Father," he said. "Only Simeon and Levi—"

"Silence!" said Jacob. "What then are these spoils you have taken? Do you not benefit from the slaughter as much as they who carried it out? Your guilt is equal to theirs—greater, for you had more wisdom and less ferocity given you by God. You have betrayed His gifts and Him. And me also," he added, "for how dared you do this without consulting me?"

"We spared you knowledge of it, Father," said Dan, "to spare you also any guilt."

"I carry the guilt of you all," Jacob answered in the voice of an old man.

When they had gone, he gathered himself together and turned to the crowd of despairing women.

"Daughters of Salem," he said unsteadily, "few words have I for you. What you have passed through this day at the hands of my sons will be my burden, and yours, forever. But thus it is. Your lives, and your children's lives, are in my hands now. I who have fathered wild beasts am no beast myself. Trust me to deal gently with you. Choose new husbands, if you can, from among the men of my people, and it shall be my especial charge to see that you and yours are well cared for from this day forward. With each shall go the flocks that belonged to your dead men."

A moan like the wind before a storm swept the crowd, and mothers clutched their little ones to them. But one, a young girl whom Simeon had been dragging along, ran to Jacob and threw herself at his feet.

"My lord, don't, I beg you, let your cruel son take me! He killed my father and my brother, and I have no one now to protect me! Your daughter was my friend. Do not give me to Simeon!"

Jacob raised her up.

"Let this be known among you all," he said. "None of you shall be forced to wed my sons against your will. Let them live without wives, for this deed today unfits them for the gentle companionship of women. Concubines they

may have, for they are destined to beget children; but your
tents shall be free of them, for, poor, simple, and despised
as you are, and bereft of all protection but mine, they are
still unworthy of you."

Sad, sad, sad were the days that followed. The men had
hardly returned to us from their purification in the desert
than Jacob ordered that all should be packed up, the herds
collected, and the tents folded, for we were to leave that
place and travel at last to our final destination in Canaan.
Flee there, rather; for we all knew that the neighboring
tribes had had word of the sacking of Salem and might be
gathering to attack us.

    We women of Jacob's tents had already been busy for
some days, assuaging our own painful sorrows by helping
to comfort and settle the widows and orphans our sons had
created. The men of our people were glad enough to take
many of them into their tents, but the less comely and
young had to seek consolation and aid from us and from
each other. Their young children were Rachel's particular
care, and she treated them most tenderly. She alone had no
weight of guilt upon her soul, for Joseph had had no part
in the slaughter.

    And I? My place was with Dinah, and I scarcely ever
left her. For days I waited for her to recover her senses.
She lay with her head in my lap, sometimes stirring, even
opening her eyes, but for the most part lying silent as one
dead. I poured milk and wine into her mouth from time to
time, that she might not die of hunger. And I held and
rocked her like a little child, and mourned her fresh, un-
stained youth that had left her forever.

    When we set off, she was still only partly conscious,
and had not spoken to me. Her eyes, when she opened
them, were blank, and her words were moans and mutter-
ings; her hands moved without purpose or strength. So I

laid her on a litter and gave her to two of our menservants
to carry, and I walked at her side as long as I could and
then rode a little to rest, then walked again.

Issachar and Zebulun crept up to me, like whipped
curs.

"Let us carry her, Mother. Let us do something."

"Be gone from my sight," I said stonily, and they
dropped back.

Rachel rode nearby on a sturdy ass. Her condition
was obvious now.

"How do you feel?" I asked her.

"Not well," she said, opening her eyes, for she rode
slumped as if asleep. "I could have wished for the birth to
come before our journey. Be with me, Leah, when my
time is upon me. I'm afraid."

"You will be all right," I said. "You are still young."

"Young?" she said with a strange laugh. I said no more.
It had been a foolish saying, for she was nearly fifty.

At a place called Beit-El, we made camp.

Jacob gathered us together—the sons were not called,
but came anyway, and stood outside the circle.

"This place was named by me," he said. "Here I set
up an altar on my journey from my home to Aram many
years ago. I called it "the House of God" because God appeared to me here, and made me certain promises and set
me a riddle in a dream, which I thought I had solved,
though I am no longer certain of that or of anything. Now
I shall rebuild the altar, and hope that God may come to
me again and renew His word to me."

So he searched for the great stone he had stood on
end as an altar, and he found it (or one like it) and stood it
up again, and piled others around it, and poured wine and
oil upon it as an offering. Then he bowed down to pray,
and we stood silent around him. Our sons crept closer, as if
feeling they might gain a little grace through being near
their father in that holy place as he prayed.

At last, after several hours, during which I felt sure my old legs would collapse under me and I longed to get back to Dinah who lay alone in my tent, Jacob stood up and turned to us. His face was alight and we all murmured, seeing that something had happened.

"All is well," he said. "God has spoken to me. His favor has not been forfeited, nor will any molest us on our way to the land of my fathers which is to be given to me. Get you to rest, for tomorrow we go on."

That night Dinah opened her eyes and knew me.

"Mother?" she said faintly.

"I am here, dear one," I said, my heart all but breaking.

"They killed him," she said softly. "They killed him before my eyes."

"It had to be so, Dinah," I said. "He dishonored you."

"But he spoke to me tenderly. He comforted me."

"Do not think of it. It is past."

She closed her eyes but still her lips moved.

"They killed him. They killed him before my eyes."

We traveled on, a sad, heavy-burdened family. Only Jacob seemed lighter in his spirit since his sojourn with God at Beit-El. He even began to speak to some of the sons again, though not to Simeon or Levi.

Each night when we stopped, he came to my tent.

"How is she?"

"No better, my lord."

"Has she spoken?"

"A little. A few words."

"She hides herself. She does not want to wake up to shame. I have heard of such things."

"It is not only shame. It is grief."

"It is not for her to be grieved," Jacob said sternly,

and left us. But love brought him back again each night to ask after her, and one night he found me weeping.

"What is it, Leah? Is she worse?"

"Her words make no sense now, my lord. She knew me before but now no longer. Oh, God, help her! What if we have destroyed her wits? Has she not lost enough without this?"

He bent over Dinah and looked at her. She was moving feebly and muttering; she looked up at him but did not see him. He straightened.

"Time may cure her," he said.

But she was beyond the help even of time.

And now another blow fell on us.

At a place called Beit-Lehem we had to stop at midday, for Rachel went into labor.

It was a long, hard struggle, do as we would to help to ease it. Her aging body, its natural strength and skill in this business forgotten, strained and strove, and Rachel was as one locked inside a chest strapped between two camels, rocking and heaving and groaning until I thought she could bear no more. As the child finally struggled forth into my hands, Rachel gave a panting cry.

"Rachel! Be strong, my sister, and don't fear, for here is another son for you, well-made and lusty. Hear how he cries! Take him in your arms and be comforted for your pain."

And I laid him on her breast, and she looked at him with her dying eyes and said, "Call him Ben-Oni, son of my sorrow." And she stretched forward her lips with the last of her strength, and kissed him, and died.

We buried her nearby, and Jacob, for whose grief there are no words, built a monument of stone over her. Joseph wept bitterly and so did I, but Jacob could not weep. He only held the new baby in his arms and said:

"A man could well turn his heart from such a child, for causing the death of such a woman as my Rachel. But not I. He was her parting gift to me, and I shall cherish him. But the name she gave him I cannot countenance, for there is enough of sorrow in me when I look at him without giving voice to it each time I call him to me. So I shall change his name to Benjamin, Son of My Right Hand." And he kissed the little face and then, handing him to me, added, "You shall rear him, Leah, for he was born into your hands. Besides, you have lost much."

So we left my sister behind us and traveled on. And now it was Benjamin I carried, as I had once carried Dinah.

There was much to do on the journey, to keep the flocks moving and together, and to keep ourselves and our livestock fed and watered. Jacob could not retain his enmity to his sons forever, for in such a situation each is dependent upon each, and every hand is needed. At first he would give his orders to his sons through other mouths, but sometimes there was an occasion of urgency when he would shout to one or another, "Do this!" "Bring that!" Before many weeks had passed, one might have thought that the slaughter at Salem had not happened—except for Dinah.

She was our reminder, our conscience. Her body recovered. Soon she could walk at my side, and eat, and drink. But her mind stayed dark. To this day, she does not suffer Simeon and Levi to come near her. Only Joseph is her companion, and in his gentle goodness plays with her sometimes, as with a little girl. Her simple love must be his comfort for the hatred I see growing up between him and his brothers, who, as I think, cannot bear his being free of blood-guiltiness.

To me, Dinah is beloved as never before. Even Benjamin, sweet boy as he is, does not lie closer to my heart than this poor daughter, broken by the cruelty of a law that was taken too far.

Yet, despite all, she is not helpless or without skills. At this very moment, she sits cross-legged at my side, stitching, at her father's command, a beautiful coat for Joseph, the favorite of them both: a coat apart from all others, for in her confusion she knows not one color from another and is sewing color to color, as a child gathers desert flowers at random in the spring.

LYNNE REID BANKS *was born in London, the daughter of a Scottish doctor and an Irish actress. She spent the war years as an evacuee in the Canadian prairies and on her return to England she studied acting at R.A.D.A. She was one of the first women reporters on British television, with Independent Television News; she worked with this company for seven years, subsequently as a scriptwriter. In 1961 she went to live in a kibbutz in Israel but has now returned to England. She is married to sculptor Chaim Stephenson, and they have three sons.*

Her first novel, THE L-SHAPED ROOM, *was a best seller and was later made into a film. Her other books include* AN END TO RUNNING, CHILDREN AT THE GATE, THE BACKWARD SHADOW, TWO IS LONELY, *and* ONE MORE RIVER, *a novel for young adults.*